Autism & PDD™
Basic
Reading
Comprehension
Kit

Pam Britton Reese
Nena C. Challenner

Skill Areas:	reading comprehension, vocabulary
Ages:	5 thru 12
Grades:	K thru 7

LinguiSystems®

LinguiSystems, Inc.
3100 4th Avenue
East Moline, IL 61244-9700
1-800 PRO IDEA
1-800-776-4332

FAX: 1-800-577-4555
E-mail: service@linguisystems.com
Web: www.linguisystems.com
TDD: 1-800-933-8331
         (for those with hearing impairments)

Copyright © 2003 LinguiSystems, Inc.

Printed in the U.S.A.

ISBN 0-7606-0495-9

About the Authors

Pam Britton Reese, M.A., CCC-SLP, owns a private practice, CommunicAid Plus, where she provides speech and language services to children and adults. She is also an educational consultant to public and private schools in Texas. *Autism & PDD: Basic Reading Comprehension Kit* is her seventh publication with LinguiSystems.

Nena C. Challenner, M.Ed., is an assistant principal at Long-branch Elementary School in Midlothian, Texas. She has over 20 years of experience in general and special education. *Autism & PDD: Basic Reading Comprehension Kit* is her sixth publication with LinguiSystems.

About this Book

Good readers organize new words by connecting them to previously learned words or ideas for future retrieval. Children with autism lack the ability to organize new information with existing knowledge. Each word in the *Dictionary* can be looked up for the meaning (in text) and/or for the category (in picture format). The definitions and sample sentences will help the child attach meaning to the word. By placing the dictionary pictures into categories, we are hoping to create a "semantic organizer" (Twachtman 1995, p. 147) to help the child with autism organize new vocabulary and concepts.

Edited by Lauri Whiskeyman, Illustrations by Margaret Warner,
Page Layout by Christine Buysse, Cover Design by Mike Paustian

Table of Contents

Animal Sounds

baa

cock-a-doodle-doo

gobble

grrr

hee-haw

honk

meow

moo

neigh

oink

quack

ribbit

Sssss

tweet

whoo

woof

Animals: Birds

bluebird

canary

cardinal

crow

duck

eagle

goose

hummingbird

ostrich

owl

parakeet

Animals: Birds, *continued*

parrot

peacock

pelican

penguin

pigeon

robin

seagull

sparrow

swan

woodpecker

Animals: Farm Animals

chicken

cow

donkey

goat

hen

horse

lamb

pig

pony

rooster

sheep

turkey

Animals: Fish and Other Ocean Animals

Fish

eel

fish

sailfish

salmon

shark

tuna

Other Ocean Animals

crab

dolphin

jellyfish

octopus

shrimp

starfish

stingray

whale

Animals: Forest Animals

bear

beaver

chipmunk

deer

fox

opossum

raccoon

skunk

squirrel

wolf

Animals: Insects

ant

bee

beetle

butterfly

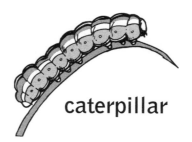

caterpillar

cricket

fly

grasshopper

ladybug

mosquito

Animals: Mammals

bat

camel

elephant

gorilla

giraffe

hippopotamus

kangaroo

koala

leopard

lion

Animals: Mammals, *continued*

monkey

mouse

panda

porcupine

rat

reindeer

rhinoceros

seal

tiger

zebra

Animals: Pets

cat

dog

gerbil

goldfish

hamster

kitten

puppy

rabbit

Animals: Reptiles and Amphibians

Reptiles

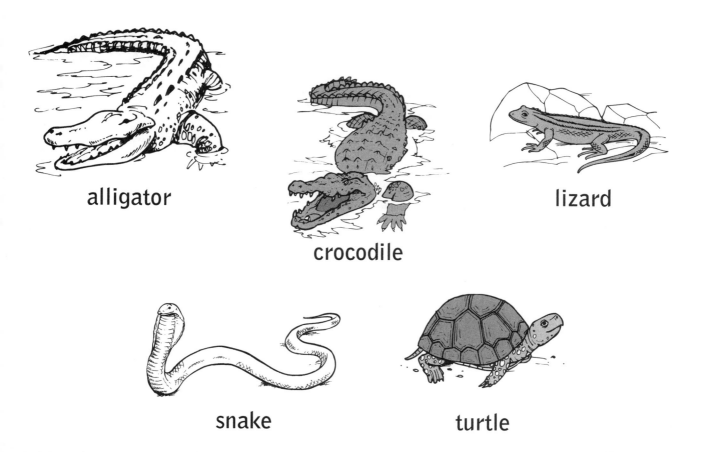

alligator

crocodile

lizard

snake

turtle

Amphibians

frog

salamander

toad

Body Parts

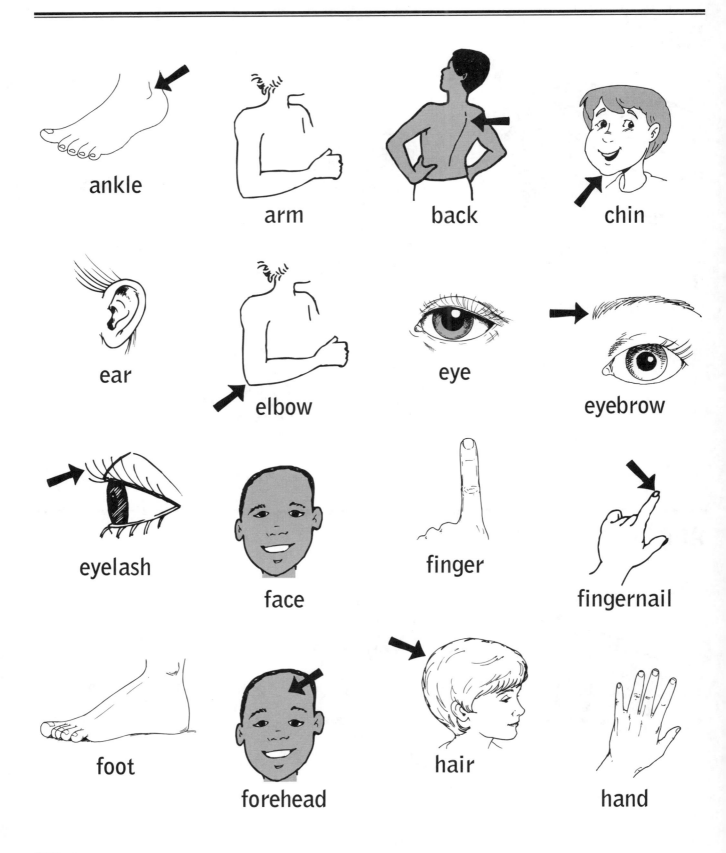

ankle

arm

back

chin

ear

elbow

eye

eyebrow

eyelash

face

finger

fingernail

foot

forehead

hair

hand

Body Parts, *continued*

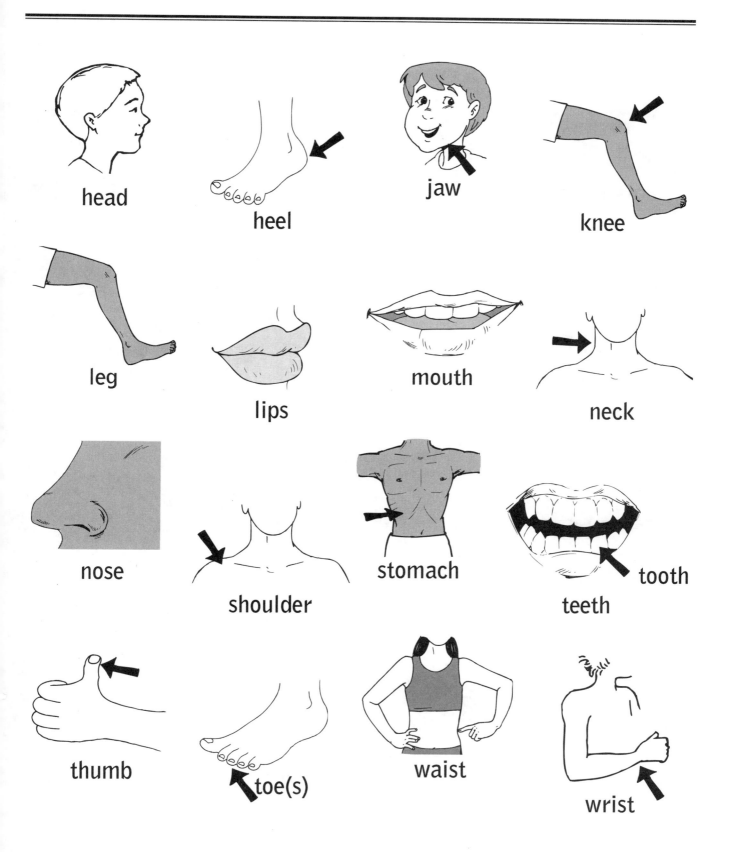

head

heel

jaw

knee

leg

lips

mouth

neck

nose

shoulder

stomach

teeth

tooth

thumb

toe(s)

waist

wrist

Breads

bagel

biscuit

bun

SALTINES

cracker

doughnut

English muffin

loaf

muffin

pancake

pita

pretzel

roll

slice

toast

tortilla

waffle

Clothing

coat

dress

gloves

hat

jacket

mittens

pajamas

pants

shirt

shoes

shorts

skirt

socks

sweater

T-shirt

vest

Colors

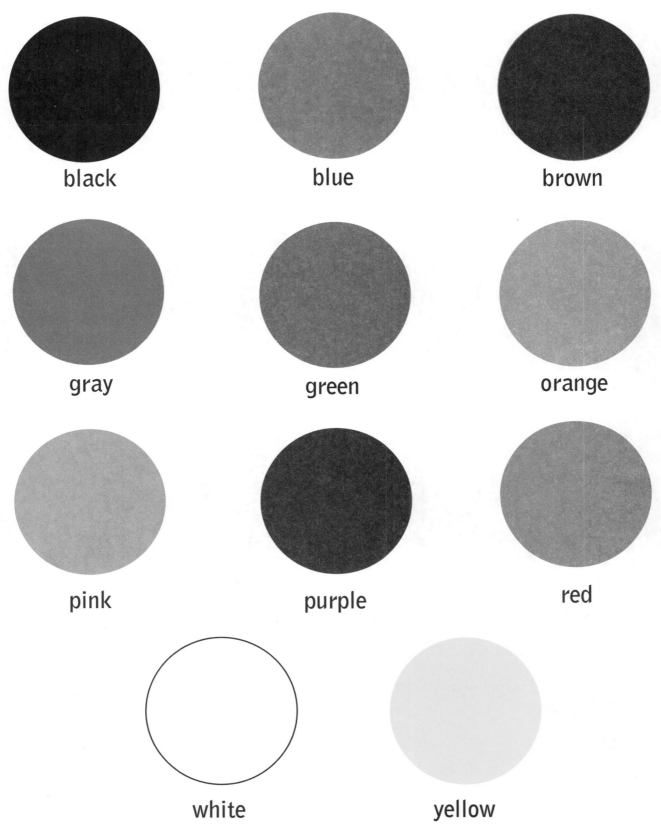

black

blue

brown

gray

green

orange

pink

purple

red

white

yellow

Community Workers

baker

barber

carpenter

cook

dentist

doctor

electrician

firefighter

librarian

mail carrier

mechanic

nurse

painter

police officer

teacher

waitress

Cooking Utensils

baster

bowl

can opener

fork

grater

knife

measuring cup

pastry brush

peeler

potato masher

scraper

spatula

spoon

tongs

whisk

Dairy

butter

cheese

cottage cheese

cream cheese

ice cream

milk

yogurt

Days of the Week

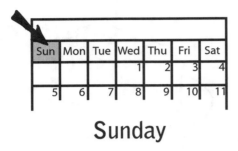

Sunday

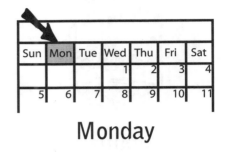

Monday

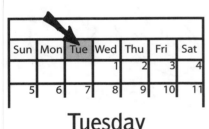

Tuesday

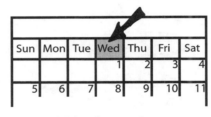

Wednesday

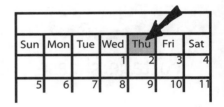

Thursday

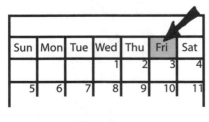

Friday

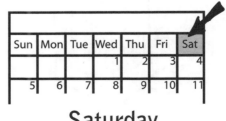

Saturday

Describing Words

another

beautiful

big

clean

cold

dark

dirty

early

easy

1+1 = ___

fast

fat

funny

Describing Words, *continued*

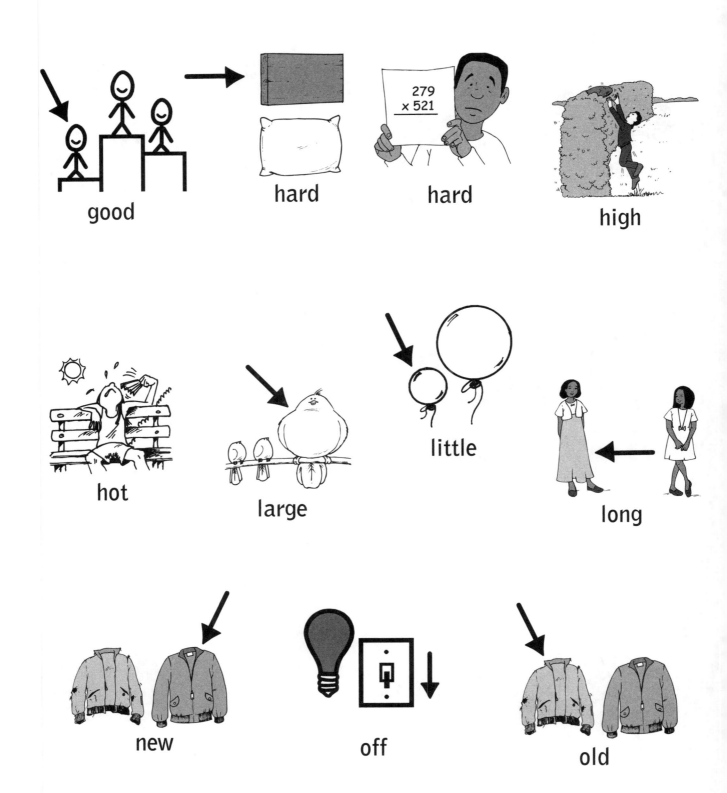

good

hard

hard

high

hot

large

little

long

new

off

old

Describing Words, *continued*

on

pretty

sharp

short

slick

slow

small

soft

tall

ugly

warm

Family

aunt

brother

cousin

daughter

father

grandfather

grandmother

husband

mother

sister

son

uncle

wife

Feelings

afraid

angry

bashful

bored

embarrassed

excited

guilty

happy

hope

jealous

love

proud

sad

sorry

surprised

tired

Fruit

apple

banana

blueberries

cantaloupe

cherry

grapes

lemon

lime

mango

orange

peach

pear

pineapple

plum

strawberry

watermelon

Household Items

bathtub

bed

chair

computer

couch

dresser

lamp

microwave

mirror

mop

refrigerator

sink

stove

table

telephone

television

toilet

How Much/How Many

0   1   2   3   4   5

zero   one   two   three   four   five

6   7   8   9   10

six   seven   eight   nine   ten

a little/a lot

all/none

empty/full

few/many

penny

nickel

dime

quarter

dollar

Meats

bacon

bologna

chicken

crab

egg

fish

ham

hamburger

hot dog

pork chop

salmon

sausage

steak

tuna

turkey

Months of the Year

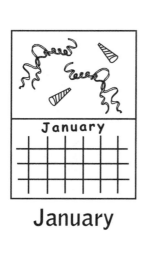

January

February

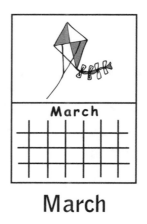

March

April

May

June

July

August

September

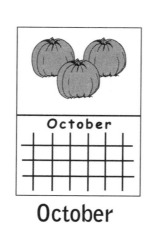

October

November

December

Musical Instruments

banjo

clarinet

drum

flute

French horn

guitar

harmonica

piano

saxophone

trombone

trumpet

tuba

violin

xylophone

People

boy

girl

man

men

woman

women

Personal and Miscellaneous Items

Personal Items

brush

comb

watch

Miscellaneous Items

bath

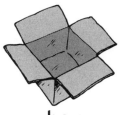
box

button

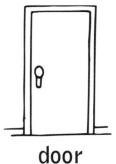
door

drink

home

house

present

water

Places in the Community

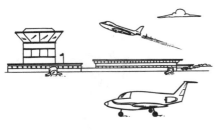

airport

apartment

bakery

drugstore

factory

fire station

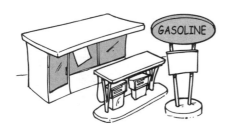

gas station

grocery store

hospital

Places in the Community, *continued*

library

neighborhood

office

park

play

post office

restaurant

school

town

Plants

bark

bulb

bush

flower

grass

leaf

petal

plant

root

seed

stem

tree

vine

Pronouns

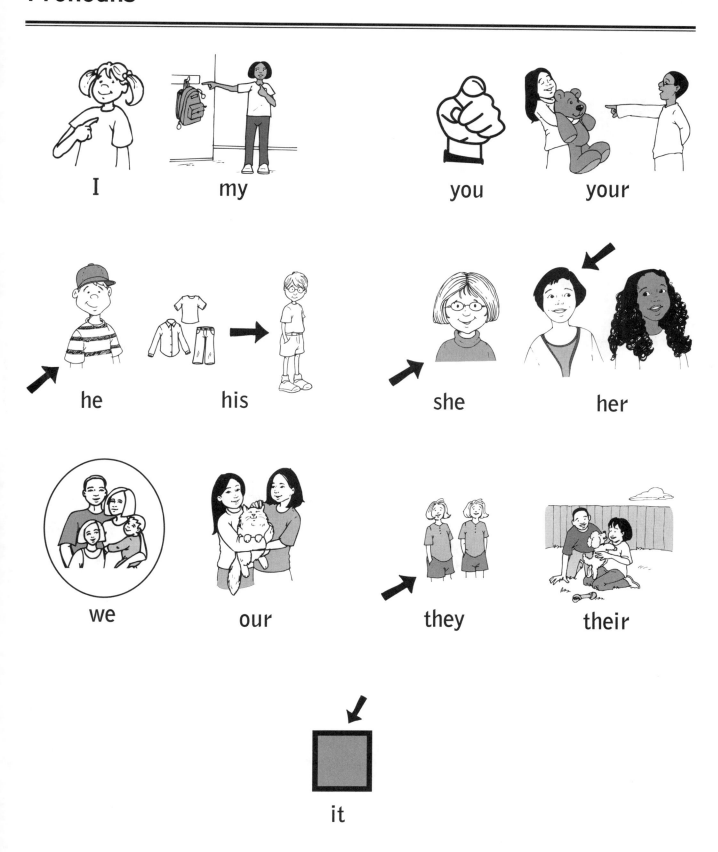

I   my   you   your

he   his   she   her

we   our   they   their

it

School

backpack

bell

book

chair

clay

clock

crayons

desk

folder

glue

marker(s)

notebook

paper

pen

pencil

ruler

Seasons

spring

summer

fall

winter

Sequence Words

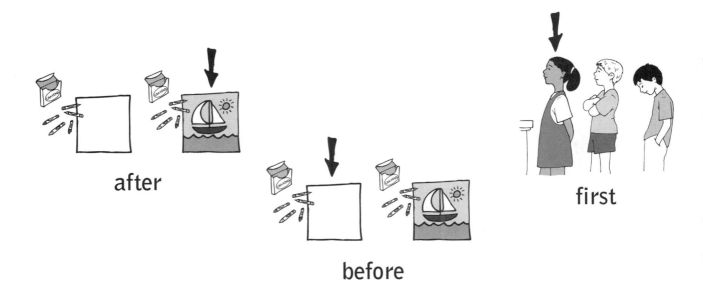

after

before

first

last

next

second

third

Shapes

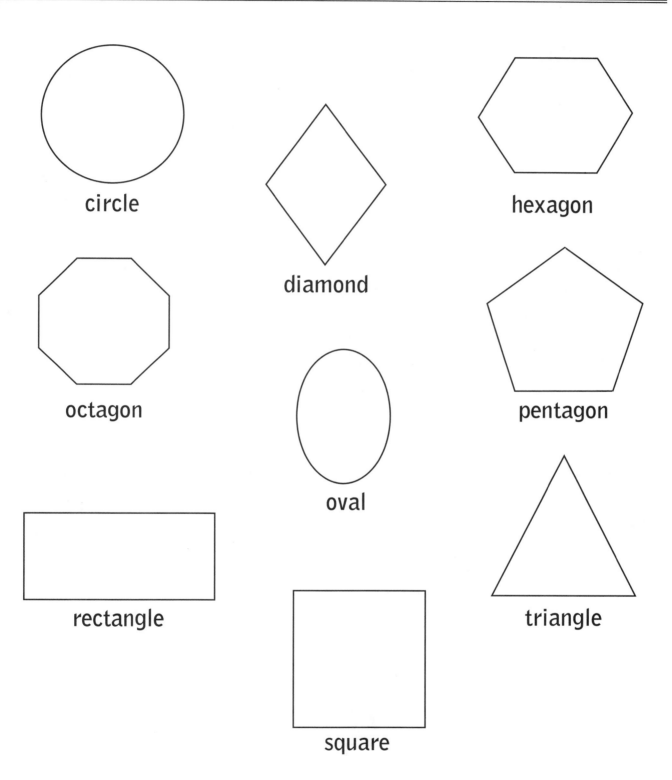

circle

diamond

hexagon

octagon

oval

pentagon

rectangle

square

triangle

Story Characters

dragon

elf

fairy

ghost

giant

king

pirate

prince

princess

queen

troll

unicorn

witch

wizard

Things to Read

book

card

comics

label

letter

letters

list

magazine

newspaper

recipe

sign

Tools

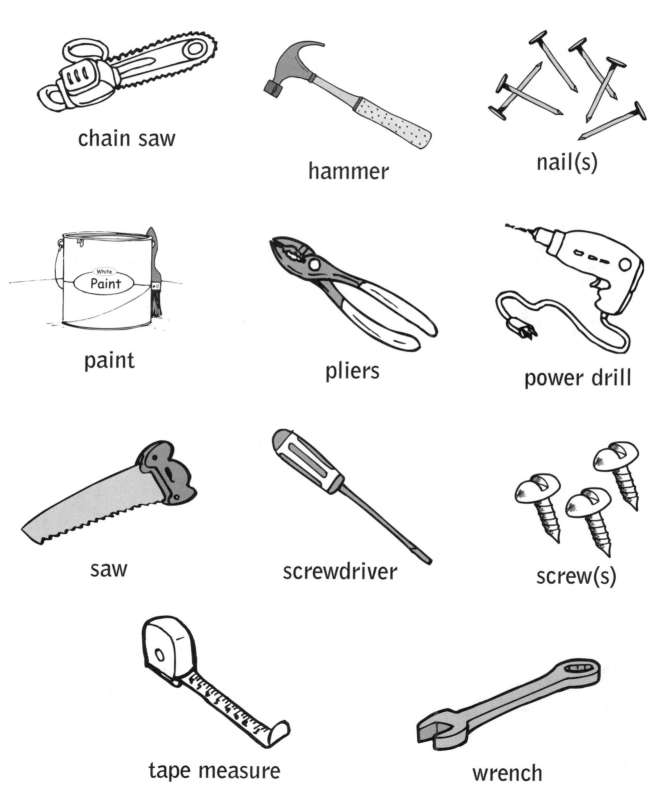

chain saw

hammer

nail(s)

paint

pliers

power drill

saw

screwdriver

screw(s)

tape measure

wrench

Toys

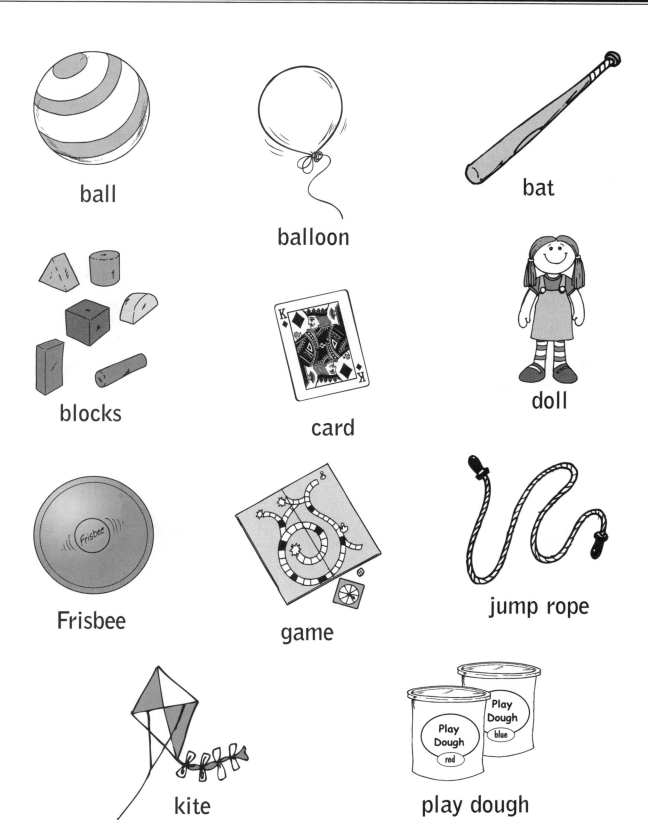

ball

balloon

bat

blocks

card

doll

Frisbee

game

jump rope

kite

play dough

puppet

puzzle

skateboard

skates

slide

stuffed animal

swing

wagon

whistle

yo-yo

Transportation

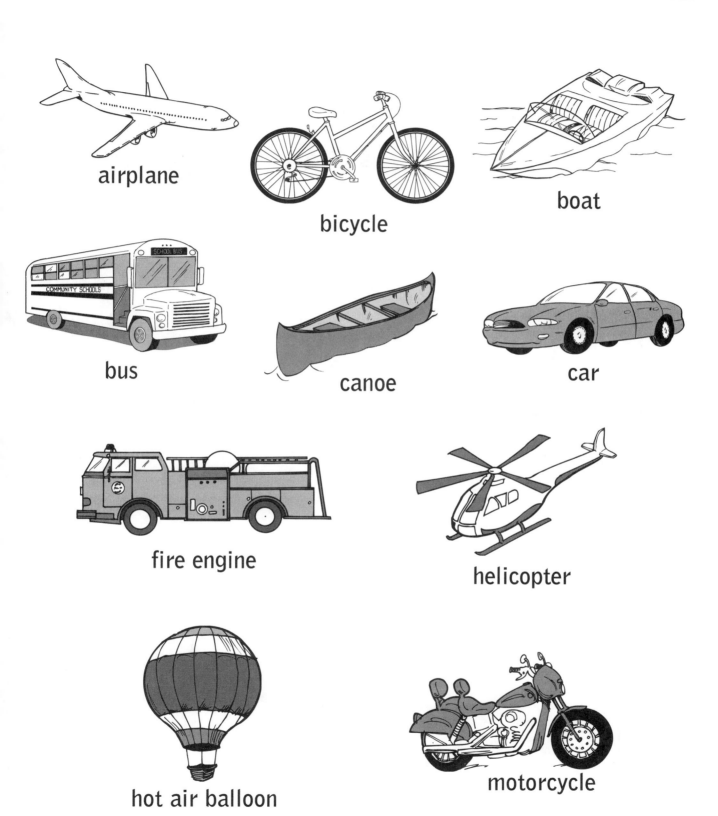

airplane

bicycle

boat

bus

canoe

car

fire engine

helicopter

hot air balloon

motorcycle

rocket

sail

sailboat

ship

submarine

subway

taxi

train

tricycle

truck

Vegetables

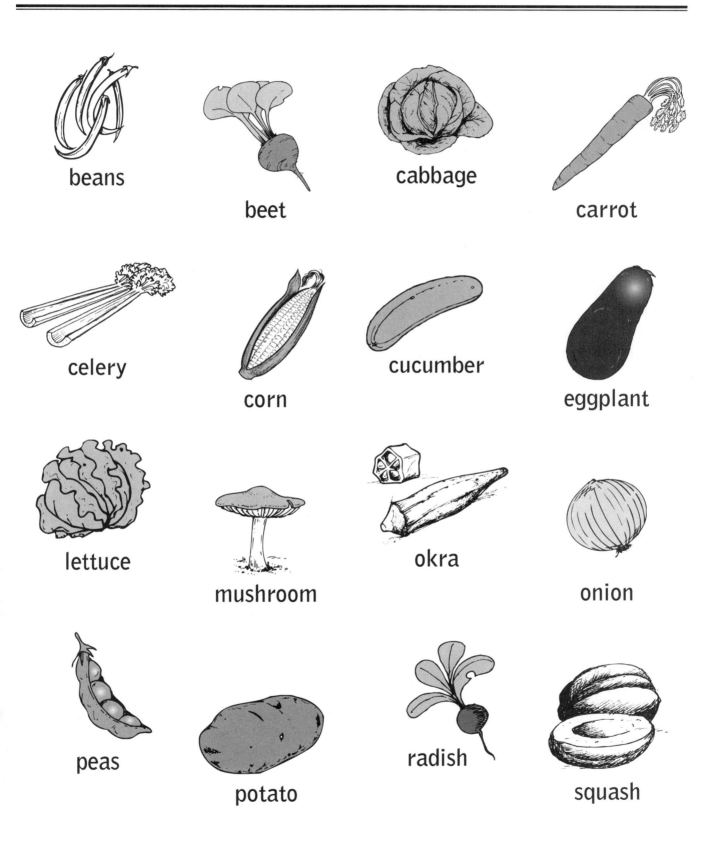

beans

beet

cabbage

carrot

celery

corn

cucumber

eggplant

lettuce

mushroom

okra

onion

peas

potato

radish

squash

Verbs

answer

ask

bake

bark

be

bite

blow

break

bring

brush

build

button

buy

Verbs, *continued*

call

carry

catch

choose

clean

climb

close

color

comb

come

cook

cry

cut

dance

Verbs, continued

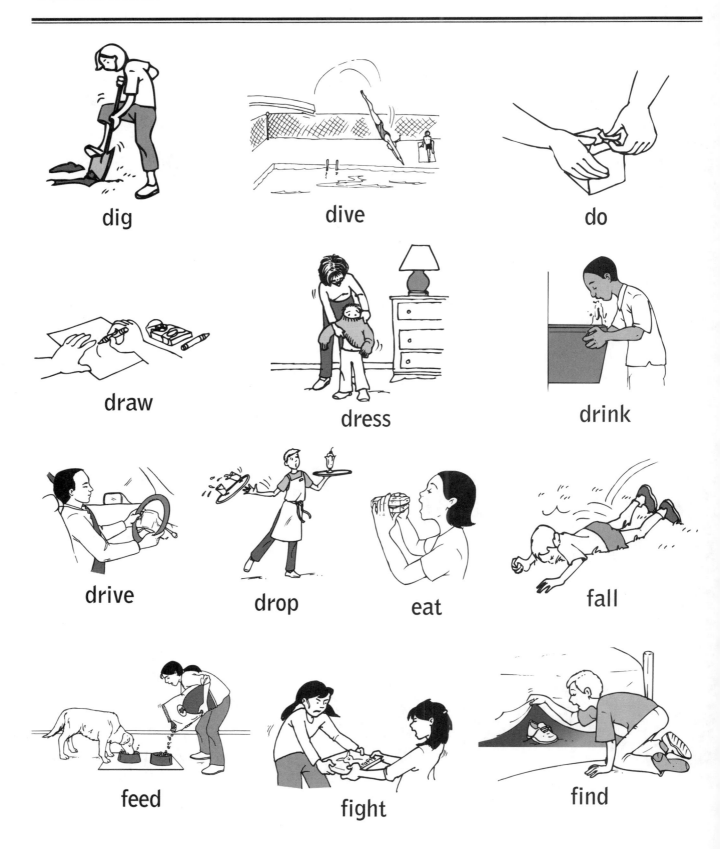

dig

dive

do

draw

dress

drink

drive

drop

eat

fall

feed

fight

find

Verbs, *continued*

fish

fix

fly

fold

follow

forget

get

give

glue

go

grow

hammer

have

hear

Verbs, *continued*

help

hide

hit

hold

honk

hurt

jump

keep

kick

know

laugh

leave

let

Verbs, continued

lick

like

live

look

lose

make

mop

move

need

open

painter

paint

plant

Verbs, *continued*

play

point

pour

print

pull

push

put

read

rest

ride

roll

run

Verbs, *continued*

sail

saw

say

scare

see

sew

shine

shovel

show

sing

sit

skate

Verbs, *continued*

sleep

slice

slide

smile

stand

start

stir

stop

sweep

swim

swing

take

Verbs, *continued*

talk

tear

tell

thank

think

throw

touch

try

turn

use

walk

want

Verbs, *continued*

wash

watch

water

wear

whistle

wink

wish

work

wrap

write

yawn

yell

Weather

breeze

cloud

hail

hurricane

ice

lightning

rain

sleet

snow

storm

sun

thunder

tornado

wind

When

afternoon

always

day

early

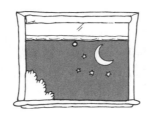
evening

late

morning

never

night

today

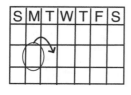
tomorrow

year

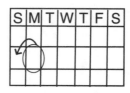
yesterday

Where

above

across

ahead

around

at

back

behind

below

beside

between

by

down

Where, *continued*

end

far

front

high

in

indoors

inside

into

low

near

off

on

Where, *continued*

out

outdoors

outside

over

to

under

underneath

up

upon

upstairs

Which One?

her

him

me

mine

them

us

that

this

these

left

right

a little   A little means just one or two or a small amount. *There is only* ***a little*** *bit left in the bowl.* p. 32

a lot   A lot means several or many. It also means a large amount of something. *She ate* ***a lot*** *of candy at the party.* p. 32

above   Above means over or higher than. *The clouds are* ***above*** *me in the sky.* p. 67

across   a. Across means on the other side. *She lives* ***across*** *the street.* p. 67
         b. Across means from one side to the other. *I will walk* ***across*** *the street.* p. 67

afraid   Afraid is a feeling. Some people are afraid, or frightened, of the dark. *My sister is* ***afraid*** *of dogs.* p. 29

after   After means at a later time. *I will take my turn* ***after*** *you.* p. 44

afternoon   Afternoon is part of a day. Afternoon is from 12:00 noon until night. *School is over in the* ***afternoon***. p. 66

ahead   Ahead means in front. *She will walk* ***ahead*** *of me and get to the house first.* p. 67

airplane   An airplane is a way to travel. People fly in an airplane. *We will travel in an* ***airplane*** *to visit Grandma.* p. 51

airport   An airport is a place where airplanes take off and land. People go to an airport to get on airplanes. *We will pick up Grandma at the* ***airport***. p. 38

all   All means every one. ***All*** *of the children will go to the zoo. No one will stay at school.* p. 32

alligator   An alligator is an animal that lives near water. An alligator is a reptile. It is long and has sharp teeth. *I saw an* ***alligator*** *at the zoo.* p. 15

always   Always means all the time; every time. *He* ***always*** *goes to bed at 8:30.* p. 66

angry   Angry is a feeling. Some people feel angry, or mad, when they don't get what they want. *That boy took my toy. I am* ***angry***. p. 29

ankle   An ankle is part of your body. It is at the bottom of your leg, above your foot. A person has two ankles. Ankles help us walk. *My socks cover my* ***ankles***. p. 16

another　　　Another means one more or a different one. *I want **another** cookie.* p. 25

answer　　　The answer is what you say when someone asks you a question. *Please **answer** the question.* p. 54

ant　　　An ant is a very small insect. Many ants live together in an anthill. *An **ant** crawled over the rock.* p. 11

apartment　　　Some people live in an apartment. There are many apartments in one building. *My friend lives in an **apartment**.* p. 38

apple　　　An apple is a fruit. An apple can be red, green, or yellow. Apples grow on trees. *I want an **apple** for my snack.* p. 30

April　　　April is a month of the year. April is the fourth month of the year. *My birthday is on **April** 9.* p. 34

arm　　　An arm is part of your body. It is attached to your shoulder. A person has two arms. We hug and carry things with our arms. *I carried the towels in my **arms**.* p. 16

around　　　Around means on all sides or in all directions. *The fence goes **around** the yard.* p. 67

ask　　　Ask means to try to find out information. ***Ask** her what her name is.* p. 54

at　　　a. At means in or on. *They were not **at** home. I stood **at** the top of the hill.* p. 67
　　　b. At has to do with time. *The show started **at** 1:00.* p. 67

August　　　August is a month of the year. August is the eighth month of the year. It is usually hot in August. *Jake's birthday is in **August**.* p. 34

aunt　　　An aunt is a female person in your family. She is your mother's or father's sister. ***Aunt** Maria is coming to visit.* p. 28

baa   "Baa" is the sound a sheep makes. *When I went in the barn, I heard the sheep "baa."* p. 5

back   a. A back is part of the body. It is below your neck and above your bottom. *People pat me on the back.* p. 16

b. Back is a place to be or a position. *He walked to the back of the line.* p. 67

backpack   A backpack is a bag that you wear on your back. A backpack holds things you need to carry. *I put books in my backpack.* p. 42

bacon   Bacon is a food. Bacon is a meat. *I like to eat bacon and eggs for breakfast.* p. 33

bagel   A bagel is a food. A bagel is a bread. It is round like a doughnut. *I ate a bagel for breakfast.* p. 18

bake   Bake means to cook something in the oven. *I like to bake cakes.* p. 54

baker   A baker is a person. A baker bakes bread and cakes. *The baker makes bread every morning.* p. 21

bakery   A bakery is a place where people buy breads and cakes. *We ordered Grandma's birthday cake from the bakery.* p. 38

ball   A ball is a toy. It is usually round. People use a ball to play games like baseball and soccer. *Let's get the ball and play basketball.* p. 49

balloon   A balloon is a toy. It is stretchy. People blow up balloons for decorations. *I got a red balloon at the circus.* p. 49

banana   A banana is a fruit. A banana is long and yellow. You peel a banana before you eat it. *I had a banana in my lunch.* p. 30

banjo   A banjo is a musical instrument. A banjo has strings. You play a banjo with your hands. *At the party, the man played a banjo.* p. 35

barber   A barber is a person. A barber's job is to cut hair. *The barber cut my hair.* p. 21

bark   a. A bark is a sound that dogs make. It sounds like "woof-woof" or "arf-arf." *My dog barks when he sees me.* p. 54

b. Bark is part of a tree. The brown part on the trunk and branches is called the bark. *The bark on the tree was rough.* p. 40

bashful	Bashful is a feeling. Some people feel bashful, or shy, when they meet new people. *I felt **bashful** when I went to my new school.* p. 29
baster	A baster is a cooking tool. A baster squirts liquid on food. *The cook used a **baster** on the turkey.* p. 22
bat	a. A bat is an animal. A bat is a mammal. A bat flies at night. *The **bats** flew into the cave.* p. 12 b. A bat is a wooden stick. You use a bat to hit a ball when you play baseball. *It's my turn, so please hand me the **bat**.* p. 49
bath	A bath is when you sit in a bathtub full of warm water. You wash your body when you take a bath. *The boy took a **bath** after he played outside.* p. 37
bathtub	A bathtub is in the bathroom of a house. People fill a bathtub with water and then sit in it to wash or take a bath. *I will get in the **bathtub** and take a bath.* p. 31
be **(am, are, been, is, was, were)**	a. Be means to have life. *I will **be** 10 years old next week.* p. 54 b. Be means to stay or to go. *We are going to **be** late.* p. 54
beans	Beans are a food. Beans are a vegetable. *We took baked **beans** to eat at the picnic.* p. 53
bear	A bear is an animal. A bear is a mammal. A bear is very big and has black, brown, or white fur. *The **bear** caught a fish in the river.* p. 10
beautiful	Beautiful means pretty. Beautiful things can be pleasing to look at or hear. *The flowers were **beautiful**. She played a **beautiful** song on the piano.* p. 25
beaver	A beaver is an animal. A beaver is a mammal. Beavers live near the water. Beavers use wood to build dams for their homes. *The **beaver** swam in the water.* p. 10
bed	A bed is a piece of furniture. You sleep on a bed. *When it is time to go to sleep, I get into my **bed**.* p. 31
bee	A bee is an insect. Some bees make honey. Some bees sting people. A bee flies and says "buzz-buzz." *The **bee** landed on a flower in the garden.* p. 11
beet	A beet is food. A beet is a vegetable. It grows under the ground. Beets are purple or red. *We planted **beets** in the garden.* p. 53

beetle	A beetle is an insect. A beetle has six legs and wings. *The **beetle** crawled across the log.* p. 11
before	Before means at an earlier time. *I must finish my lunch **before** I eat dessert.* p. 44
behind	Behind means at the back of. *He will stand **behind** me in line.* p. 67
bell	A bell makes noise. A bell sound is "ring-ring." A bell rings at school when it is time to go home. *My bicycle has a **bell** on the handlebars.* p. 42
below	Below means beneath. *From the tree, I could see my friend **below**.* p. 67
beside	Beside means next to. *My brother will sit **beside** me.* p. 67
between	Between means in the space separating two things or people. *In art class I sit **between** Maria and Jack.* p. 67
bicycle	A bicycle is a way to travel. A bicycle has two wheels. You ride a bicycle by pedaling to make the wheels turn. *"Bike" is a short name for **bicycle**.* p. 51
big	Big means large or very important. *An elephant is a very **big** animal.* p. 25
biscuit	A biscuit is a food. A biscuit is a bread. *I eat **biscuits** at breakfast.* p. 18
bite (bit)	Bite means to cut into with teeth. *Take a **bite** of your food.* p. 54
black	Black is a color. The sky is black at night. *My dog is **black** and white.* p. 20
blocks	Blocks are a toy. Blocks are cubes made out of wood or plastic. Children stack blocks to make things. *I like to build houses with my **blocks**.* p. 49
blow (blew)	Blow means to move or shape something with air. *It is fun to **blow** bubbles.* p. 54
blue	Blue is a color. The sky is blue. *Laura has **blue** eyes.* p. 20
blueberry	A blueberry is a fruit. Blueberries grow on bushes. ***Blueberry** muffins are my favorite.* p. 30
bluebird	A bluebird is an animal. A bluebird is a bird that has blue feathers. *A **bluebird** flew near the window.* p. 6

boat	A boat is a way to travel. People ride in a boat on the water. *I ride in a boat when we go fishing.* p. 51
bologna	Bologna is a food. Bologna is a meat. People make sandwiches with bologna. *I made a bologna sandwich for lunch.* p. 33
book	A book is something to read. A book has a cover and pages with words. Some books have pictures. *We read a book every night at bedtime.* pp. 42, 47
bored	Bored is a feeling. People feel bored when they have nothing to do. *Sometimes I am bored when my favorite TV show is not on.* p. 29
bowl	A bowl is a dish. People eat soup, cereal, or ice cream from a bowl. *Luke ate a bowl of soup for dinner.* p. 22
box	A box holds things. A box is made of cardboard. It is a square or rectangle shape. Some boxes have lids. *Please open the box of crackers.* p. 37
boy	A boy is a male child. *The boy played baseball at recess.* p. 36
break (broke)	Break means to come apart by force. *The glass might break if I drop it on the floor.* p. 54
breeze	A breeze is a gentle wind. *The breeze feels cool on my skin.* p. 65
bring (brought)	Bring means to take or carry something to a place. *Please bring me a glass of water.* p. 54
brother	A brother is a person in a family. A brother is a boy. Brothers and sisters are part of the same family. *My brother and I share a room.* p. 28
brown	Brown is a color. Wood is brown. *My sister has brown hair.* p. 20
brush	a. A brush is a grooming tool. You use a brush to make your hair neat. *She put the brush in the bathroom.* p. 37 b. Brush means to scrub or smooth. *I will brush my hair before I go to school.* p. 54
build (built)	Build means to make by putting parts together. *The men will build a new house.* p. 54

bulb   A bulb is part of a plant. You put a bulb in the ground to grow a new plant. *We planted tulip **bulbs**.* p. 40

bun   A bun is food. A bun is bread. *I put my hamburger on a **bun** and ate it.* p. 18

bus   A bus is a way to travel. It is a large vehicle that many people can ride on at the same time. *I ride the **bus** to school with friends.* p. 51

bush   A bush is a plant. A bush is smaller than a tree. *That **bush** has yellow flowers in the springtime.* p. 40

butter   Butter is a food. Butter is yellow. It can come in a stick or a small container called a tub. People put butter on foods like bread, potatoes, and corn to make them taste better. *He put **butter** on his pancakes.* p. 23

butterfly   A butterfly is an insect. A butterfly flies and has colorful wings. *A **butterfly** flew near the flowers.* p. 11

button   a. A button is part of clothes. A button holds clothing together. A button is usually small and round. *My sweater has four **buttons** on it.* p. 37
                  b. Button means to fasten clothing together with a button and a buttonhole. *Mom helped Cole **button** his shirt.* p. 54

buy   Buy means to pay money for something. *We need to **buy** more milk.* p. 54
(bought)

by   By means close to. *He will sit **by** me.* p. 67

cabbage   Cabbage is a food. Cabbage is a vegetable. Cabbage is round and has green or red leaves. *We grew **cabbage** in our garden.* p. 53

call   Call means to telephone. *I need to **call** my friend on the telephone.* p. 55

camel   A camel is an animal. A camel is a mammal. A camel has one or two humps. *The **camel** walked across the desert.* p. 12

can opener   A can opener is a kitchen utensil or appliance. A can opener opens the lid on cans. *She opened the can of soup with a **can opener**.* p. 22

canary   A canary is an animal. A canary is a bird. A canary is yellow. *We have a pet **canary**.* p. 6

canoe   A canoe is a way to travel on water. It is a long, narrow boat and is usually pointed on both ends. You move it with a paddle. *They went down the river in a **canoe**.* p. 51

cantaloupe   A cantaloupe is a fruit. It is a type of melon. A cantaloupe is round and is orange inside. *I ate a slice of **cantaloupe** with my sandwich at lunch.* p. 30

car   A car is a way to travel. A car has four wheels. People ride in a car. *My neighbor got a new **car**.* p. 51

card   a. A card is something to read. It is a folded rectangle of paper with words or pictures printed on it. People send cards to friends for birthdays or holidays. *Aunt Jane sent me a **card** for my birthday.* p. 47
b. Cards are small, flat rectangles of paper with words or numbers printed on them. Some games are played with cards. *They played **cards** at the table.* p. 49

cardinal   A cardinal is an animal. A cardinal is a bird. A male cardinal is red. A female cardinal is brown. *I saw a **cardinal** at the bird feeder.* p. 6

carpenter   A carpenter is a person. A carpenter's job is to make things out of wood. *A **carpenter** made our new bookshelves.* p. 21

carrot   A carrot is a food. A carrot is a vegetable. It grows under the ground. A carrot is long, pointed, and orange. *Sometimes I eat **carrot** sticks for a snack.* p. 53

carry
(carried)   Carry means to hold something while moving it. *Please help me **carry** the boxes.* p. 55

cat

A cat is an animal. A cat is a mammal. A cat is furry and says "meow." *My cat purrs when I pet it.* p. 14

catch
(caught)

Catch means to get hold of something that is moving. *I will throw the ball and you can catch it.* p. 55

caterpillar

A butterfly or moth lays an egg. A caterpillar hatches from the egg. It looks like a worm. A caterpillar makes a cocoon and changes into a butterfly or moth. *The caterpillar ate a leaf.* p. 11

celery

Celery is a food. Celery is a vegetable. Celery is long, green, and crisp. *When I eat celery, it makes a crunching sound.* p. 53

chain saw

A chain saw is a tool. It has a motor and very sharp blades. *The man cut the wood with a chain saw.* p. 48

chair

A chair is a piece of furniture. You sit on a chair. *My brother always sits in the same chair in the living room.* pp. 31, 42

cheese

Cheese is a food. It is made from milk. Cheese can be white, yellow, or orange. Some people eat cheese on sandwiches or crackers. *I put cheese on my sandwich.* p. 23

cherry

A cherry is a fruit. Cherries are small, red, and round. They have pits in the center. Cherries grow on trees. *Cherry pie is my favorite.* p. 30

chicken

a. A chicken is an animal. A chicken is a bird. A chicken lives on a farm and lays eggs. *There were chickens on their farm.* p. 8
b. Chicken is a food. Chicken is a meat. *We ate fried chicken for supper last night.* p. 33

chin

A chin is part of your body. Your chin is on your face. Your chin is below your mouth and above your neck. *I rest my chin on my hand when I am tired.* p. 16

chipmunk

A chipmunk is a small animal that lives in a tree. A chipmunk is a mammal. A chipmunk is brown and has a black stripe on its back and tail. *The chipmunk ate a nut.* p. 10

choose
(chose)

Choose means to decide between two or more things. *You can have a sandwich or a hot dog. Which one do you choose?* p. 55

circle

A circle is a shape. A circle is round. *I drew a circle on the paper.* p. 45

clarinet	A clarinet is a musical instrument shaped like a tube. You play a clarinet by blowing into it. *My sister is learning to play the **clarinet**.* p. 35
clay	Clay is a special kind of dirt. It is easily shaped when it is wet. It becomes hard when it is dried or baked. You use clay to make pots or statues. *We used **clay** in art class.* p. 42
clean	a. Clean means uncluttered, neat, not dirty. *After I painted, I put on a **clean** shirt.* p. 25
	b. Clean means to make something messy or dirty look better. *You need to **clean** your room.* p. 55
climb	Climb means to go up using the hands and feet. *I will **climb** the ladder to the top of the slide.* p. 55
clock	A clock tells what time it is. Some clocks have hands and numbers. Some clocks have only numbers. *My classroom at school has a **clock** on the wall.* p. 42
close	Close means to shut. *Please **close** the door.* p. 55
clothing	Clothing is what we wear on our bodies. Shirts, pants, shorts, and dresses are clothing. *She put the winter **clothing** away.* p. 19
cloud	A cloud is in the sky. Clouds are white or gray. Sometimes clouds bring rain. *I like to look at **clouds**.* p. 65
coat	A coat is a piece of clothing. You wear a coat on top of your other clothes when it is cold outside. *I need to zip up my **coat**.* p. 19
cock-a-doodle-doo	Cock-a-doodle-doo is the sound a rooster makes. *In the morning we hear "**cock-a-doodle-doo**" from the rooster.* p. 5
cold	Cold means not hot. It means cool or chilly. *I put ice in my drink to make it **cold**.* p. 25
color	a. Color has to do with light as we see it with our eyes. Red, yellow, and blue are colors. *There are many **colors** in a rainbow.* p. 20
	b. Color means to give color to. *She liked to **color** with crayons.* p. 55

comb
  a. A comb is a tool you use to smooth your hair. It has plastic or metal teeth. *I use a **comb** to keep my hair neat.* p. 37
  b. Comb means to smooth with a comb. *I will **comb** my hair before I go to school.* p. 55

come (came)
Come means to reach a place. *My friend will **come** to my house tomorrow.* p. 55

comics
Comics have many pictures and are funny. You can read comics in the newspaper or in comic books. *I laugh at the **comics** every day in the newspaper.* p. 47

computer
A computer is a machine with large amounts of information in it. Computers have a monitor, a keyboard, and a mouse. *I can work and play games on a **computer**.* p. 31

cook
  a. A cook is a person. A cook's job is to cook food. A cook works at a restaurant and makes the food. *My uncle is a good **cook**.* p. 21
  b. Cook means to make food ready for eating by baking or frying it. *I am learning to **cook** food on the stove.* p. 55

corn
Corn is a food. Corn is a vegetable. Corn grows on a stalk and has little yellow kernels on it. ***Corn** is my favorite vegetable.* p. 53

cottage cheese
Cottage cheese is a food made from milk. Cottage cheese is white and lumpy. *I eat **cottage cheese** in a bowl with a spoon.* p. 23

couch
A couch is a piece of furniture. A couch is long and has soft cushions. More than one person can sit on a couch. *We have a **couch** in our living room.* p. 31

cousin
A cousin is a person in a family. Your aunt and uncle's children are your cousins. A cousin can be a boy or a girl. *I like to play with my **cousin** when I visit my aunt and uncle.* p. 28

cow
A cow is an animal. A cow is a mammal. A cow lives on a farm. A cow gives milk and says "moo." *We saw a lot of **cows** on the farm.* p. 8

crab
  a. Crab is a food. *We ate **crab** legs for dinner.* p. 33
  b. A crab is an animal that lives in the ocean. A crab is a crustacean. It has a hard shell and claws. Some people eat crabs. *Tim saw a **crab** on the sand.* p. 9

cracker   A cracker is a food. A cracker is a type of bread. Crackers are small and thin. Crackers are crunchy. *Sometimes I eat cheese or peanut butter on **crackers**.* p. 18

crayons   A crayon is something to draw or write with. It is made of wax. Crayons come in many different colors. *I like to color pictures with my **crayons**.* p. 42

cream cheese   Cream cheese is a food made from milk. Cream cheese is a kind of cheese. Cream cheese is white and creamy. *I eat **cream cheese** on a bagel for breakfast.* p. 23

cricket   A cricket is an insect. It can be black or brown. A cricket can hop. It makes a chirping sound by rubbing its legs together. *I like to hear the **crickets** at night.* p. 11

crocodile   A crocodile is an animal. A crocodile is a reptile with a long body. It lives near water. *A **crocodile** has sharp teeth.* p 15

crow   A crow is an animal. A crow is a black bird. A crow says "caw-caw." *The **crow** sat on the fence.* p. 6

cry
(cried)   Cry means to make tears. People often cry when they are hurt or sad. *Sometimes I **cry** when I fall down.* p. 55

cucumber   A cucumber is food. A cucumber is a vegetable that grows on a vine. A cucumber is long and green. *We had **cucumber** in our salad.* p. 53

cut   Cut means to slice or open with something sharp. *I **cut** paper and cloth with scissors. I **cut** meat with a knife.* p. 55

dance   Dance means to move your body in time to music. *I love to **dance** to the music.* p. 55

dark   Dark is when there is little or no light. *I see no light. It is **dark**.* p. *25*

daughter   A daughter is a person in a family. If a father and a mother have a girl child, she is a daughter. *Her **daughter** is five years old.* p. 28

day   Day starts when the sun comes up. Day is finished when the sun goes down. *We stayed at the beach all **day** on Saturday.* p. 66

December   December is the twelfth month. December is the last month in the year. Winter begins in December. *Her family took a vacation in **December**.* p. 34

deer   A deer is an animal that lives in a forest. A deer is a mammal. Some deer have antlers. *The boy fed corn to a **deer** at the petting zoo.* p. 10

dentist   A dentist is a person. A dentist's job is to keep people's teeth healthy. *The **dentist** checks my teeth twice a year.* p. 21

desk   A desk is a piece of furniture. You can write and work at a desk. *I do my homework at the **desk** in my bedroom.* p. 42

diamond   A diamond is a shape with four corners. In baseball, the lines that connect the bases make a diamond shape. *The puzzle was in the shape of a **diamond**.* p. 45

dig
(dug)   Dig means to break up or turn over dirt with your hands or a tool. *Use this shovel to **dig** a hole in the dirt.* p. 56

dime   A dime is money. A dime is a coin. A dime is worth 10 cents. *I had five **dimes** to buy some candy.* p. 32

dirty   Dirty means not clean. *My shoes have mud on them so they are **dirty**.* p. 25

dive
(dove)   Dive means to go headfirst. *Watch me **dive** into the water.* p. 56

do
(did, does)   Do means to make something or to work on something. *I need help opening the jar. Will you **do** it for me?* p. 56

doctor   A doctor is a person. A doctor's job is to help sick people get well. *When I had an earache, I went to the **doctor**.* p. 21

dog

A dog is an animal. A dog is a mammal. A dog is a pet that barks. *My dog is white with black spots.* p. 14

doll

A doll is a toy. A doll looks like a little person. *The child played with the doll.* p. 49

dollar

A dollar is paper money. It is worth 100 cents. *The book cost eight dollars.* p. 32

dolphin

A dolphin is an animal that lives in the ocean. A dolphin is a mammal. Dolphins live in the ocean. *The dolphin jumped out of the water.* p. 9

donkey

A donkey is an animal. A donkey is a mammal. It looks like a small gray horse. A donkey says "hee-haw." *We saw a donkey at the farm.* p. 8

door

A door is used to go in and out of a house or building. It is made of wood, metal, or glass. A door has a knob or handle. *Someone knocked on the door.* p. 37

doughnut

A doughnut is food. A doughnut is round and has a hole in the middle. It tastes sweet. *Sometimes I eat a doughnut for breakfast.* p. 18

down

Down means at a lower place or a direction. *The boy is up on the ladder. The girl is down on the ground.* p. 67

dragon

A dragon is a character in some stories. A dragon is not real. A dragon looks like a big lizard. *The dragon made fire come out of its mouth.* p. 46

draw
(drew)

Draw means to make lines with a tool like a crayon or a pencil. *I draw pictures with crayons or markers.* p. 56

dress

a. A dress is a type of clothing. Girls wear dresses. *She got a new dress for her birthday.* p. 19
b. Dress means to put on clothes. *I dress in the morning and put on my clothes.* p. 56

dresser

A dresser is a piece of furniture. A dresser has drawers to keep clothes in. *I put my clean clothes in the dresser in my room.* p. 31

drink
(drank)

a. A drink is a liquid to swallow when you're thirsty. *I need a drink of water.* p. 37
b. Drink means to swallow liquid. *When I am thirsty, I drink water.* p. 56

drive
(drove)
Drive means to steer a vehicle. Adults drive cars. *My mom **drives** me to school every day.* p. 56

drop
Drop means to let something fall that you are holding. *Be careful! You might **drop** the glass on the ground and break it.* p. 56

drugstore
A drugstore is a place. Adults buy medicine at a drugstore. *We got the medicine at the **drugstore**.* p. 38

drum
A drum is a musical instrument. You play a drum by hitting it with drumsticks or with your hands. *The drummer played the **drum** loudly.* p. 35

duck
A duck is an animal that can fly and swim. A duck is a bird. A duck says "quack, quack." *It is fun to feed the **ducks** at the park.* p. 6

E

eagle   An eagle is an animal. An eagle is a large bird. Bald eagles have white heads. *The **eagle** flew over the water.* p. 6

ear   An ear is a part of your body. Your ears are on your head. A person has two ears. You use your ears to hear. *The doctor looked in my **ears**.* p. 16

early   Early means before the usual time. *I got to school before it started. I was **early**.* pp. 25, 66

easy   Easy means not hard. *The work is not hard. I can do the work. The work is **easy**.* p. 25

eat
(ate)   Eat means to chew and swallow food. *I **eat** food every day.* p. 56

eel   An eel is an animal that lives in the ocean. An eel is a fish. An eel is very long and looks like a snake. *I saw an **eel** at the aquarium.* p. 9

egg   An egg is food. An egg has a hard shell that you crack. Birds lay eggs. *We had **eggs** and bacon for breakfast.* p. 33

eggplant   An eggplant is a food. An eggplant is a vegetable. *The cook chopped and cooked the **eggplant** before we ate it.* p. 53

eight   Eight is a number. Eight comes after seven. *Maria is **eight** years old.* p. 32

elbow   An elbow is a part of your body. It is between your wrist and your shoulder. A person has two elbows. Your arm bends at the elbow. *I bumped my **elbow** on the door.* p. 16

electrician   An electrician is a person. An electrician's job is to work with wires and electricity. *The **electrician** fixed our broken light.* p. 21

elephant   An elephant is an animal. An elephant is a mammal. An elephant is very big and gray and has a long trunk. *The **elephant** raised its trunk.* p. 12

elf   An elf is a character in some stories. An elf is not real. An elf is a small person. *The **elf** showed the boy where the gold was hidden.* p. 46

embarrassed   Embarrassed is a feeling. When you feel embarrassed, your face often turns red. *I was **embarrassed** that I made a mistake.* p. 29

empty   Empty means having nothing inside. *There is nothing in the box. The box is* ***empty****.* p. 32

end   End means the back of the line or when something is finished. *The last page of the story said "The **End***.*" p. 68

English   An English muffin is food. An English muffin is bread. An English muffin is
muffin   round. *I ate a toasted **English muffin** with jelly on it for breakfast.* p. 18

evening   Evening is a time of day. Evening starts when the sun goes down and it is dark outside. *Every **evening** we turn on the porch light.* p. 66

excited   Excited is a feeling. When people feel excited, they might smile or clap their hands. *I am **excited** when I get to go swimming.* p. 29

eye   An eye is part of your body. Eyes are on your face. A person has two eyes. You use your eyes to see. *I closed my **eyes****.* p. 16

eyebrow   An eyebrow is part of your body. Eyebrows are on your face. A person has two eyebrows. Eyebrows are the hair that is right above your eyes. *Mario drew eyes and **eyebrows** on the face.* p. 16

eyelash   An eyelash is part of your body. Eyelashes are on your eyes. Eyelashes are the tiny hairs that stick out from the edges of your eyelids. A person has many eyelashes. *She has long **eyelashes****.* p. 16

F

face Your face is part of your body. Your face is the front of your head. Your face has eyes, a nose, a mouth, cheeks, a chin, and a forehead on it. *I washed my face.* p. 16

factory A factory is a place. A factory is a large building where many people work to make things. *Crayons are made at a factory.* p. 38

fairy A fairy is a character in some stories. A fairy is not real. A fairy looks like a tiny person with wings. A fairy can fly. *The fairy sprinkled the flowers with special dust.* p. 46

fall
(fell)
a. Fall is a season in the year. Fall is also called autumn. Fall is when leaves turn colors and fall off the trees. *In the fall, we rake leaves.* p. 43
b. Fall means to drop or to come down quickly. *Be careful. The floor is slippery and you might fall.* p. 56

far Far is a long way. *The tree is far away. I cannot touch the tree.* p. 68

fast Fast means to move quickly. *The girl ran fast.* p. 25

fat Fat means having a lot of flesh on your body. *The pig was very fat.* p. 25

father A father is a person in a family. A father has children. He is a boy's or girl's parent. Another name for Father is Dad. *Her father picked her up from school.* p. 28

February February is a month in the year. February is the second month of the year. It is the shortest month of the year. *Valentine's Day is on February 14th.* p. 34

feed
(fed)
Feed means to give food to. *I will feed the dog.* p. 56

few Few means not many. *I only see a few candies in the bag.* p. 32

fight
(fought)
Fight means to hit or struggle. *It is not nice to fight with your friends.* p. 56

find
(found)
Find means to see something you are looking for. *Sometimes I look for something. If I see it, I find it.* p. 56

finger A finger is part of your hand. You have four fingers and a thumb on each hand. *You wear a ring on your finger.* p. 16

fingernail   A fingernail is part of your finger. You have one on the end of every finger. Your fingernails are hard. *I cut my **fingernails** with clippers to keep them short.* p. 16

fire engine   A fire engine is like a big truck. It has fire hoses and other special equipment on it. Firefighters drive a fire engine to a fire. A fire engine has a very loud siren. Some fire engines are red and some are yellow. *The **fire engine** raced through the streets to the fire.* p. 51

fire station   A fire station is a building with fire trucks in it. Firefighters live at a fire station and wait for people to call about fires. *We visited the **fire station** to learn about fire safety.* p. 38

firefighter   A firefighter is a person. A firefighter's job is to put out fires. *The **firefighter** unrolled the fire hose.* p. 21

first   First means in front of everyone. *I am **first** in line. No one is in front of me.* p. 44

fish
a. A fish is an animal that lives in water. *We saw a lot of **fish** at the pet store.* p. 9
b. Fish is a food. Fish is meat. *Sometimes I eat tuna **fish** sandwiches.* p. 33
c. Fish means to use a pole and bait to catch fish swimming in water. *I like to **fish** with my brother.* p. 57

five   Five is a number. Five comes after four. *She went to kindergarten when she was **five** years old.* p. 32

fix   Fix means to repair or make something better. *Please **fix** the broken toy.* p. 57

flower   A flower is a plant. It has a stem and a blossom. The blossoms are many different colors. Some flowers smell good. *There were **flowers** growing in the yard.* p. 40

flute   A flute is a musical instrument. It is long and silver. You play a flute by blowing into it. *The person with the **flute** played a pretty song.* p. 35

fly
(flew)
a. A fly is an insect. A fly is small and has wings. *The **fly** kept landing on the food at the picnic.* p. 11
b. Fly means to move through the air with wings. Birds and airplanes can fly in the air. *Many airplanes **fly** over my apartment building.* p. 57

fold   Fold means to bend over on itself. People fold paper and clothes. *I helped **fold** the clean clothes.* p. 57

folder	A folder is made of heavy paper and it holds other papers. Students often use folders in school. *Lee keeps his papers in a red folder.* p. 42
follow	Follow means to go after or behind. *I follow my friends when I am in line.* p. 57
foot/feet	A foot is part of your body. A person has two feet. Feet are on the bottoms of your legs. *I use my feet to stand or walk.* p. 16
forehead	A forehead is part of your body. A forehead is part of your face. *My forehead is below my hair and above my eyes.* p. 16
forget **(forgot)**	Forget means you don't remember. *Sometimes I forget to take my lunch to school.* p. 57
fork	A fork is a tool for eating. A fork has sharp points to help pick up food. *I need a fork to eat the meat.* p. 22
four	Four is a number. Four comes after three. *He ate four cookies after school.* p. 32
fox	A fox is an animal. A fox is a mammal. A fox looks like a small dog. *The fox has red fur and a bushy tail.* p. 10
French horn	A French horn is a musical instrument. A French horn is round. You play a French horn by blowing into it. *There were four people playing French horns in the band.* p. 35
Friday	Friday is a day of the week. *Next Friday we go on a field trip at school.* p. 24
Frisbee	A Frisbee is a toy. A Frisbee is flat and round and plastic. People throw and catch a Frisbee. *I watched the dog catch a Frisbee in his mouth.* p. 49
frog	A frog is an animal that lives near water. A frog is an amphibian. A frog is green and can jump high. A frog says "ribbit." *The frog jumped into the water.* p. 15
front	Front is a place to be or a position. Front is the part facing forward. *The man is painting the front of the house.* p. 68
full	Full means holding as much as possible or not empty. *My glass of water is full. There is water near the top.* p. 32
funny	Funny things make you laugh. *Clowns are very funny. They make me laugh.* p. 25

G

game
A game is something fun that people do together. Some games are played with a board and dice. *My family played a game together on Friday night.* p. 49

gas station
A gas station is a place to buy gas. *The man pulled into the gas station to put gas in his car.* p. 38

gerbil
A gerbil is an animal. A gerbil is a mammal. A gerbil is small and furry. Some people have a gerbil for a pet. *My friend has a pet gerbil.* p. 14

get
(got)
Get is when you receive something. *She will get some books at the library.* p. 57

ghost
A ghost is a character in some stories. A ghost is not real. A ghost looks hazy and is usually white. *The ghost scared the people when it said, "Boo!"* p. 46

giant
A giant is a character in some stories. A giant is not real. A giant looks like a very big person. *In the story, Jack saw a giant.* p. 46

giraffe
A giraffe is an animal that lives in Africa. A giraffe is a mammal. A giraffe has a very long neck. *I saw a giraffe at the zoo.* p. 12

girl
A girl is a female child. *That girl likes to swing.* p. 36

give
(gave)
Give means to hand over. *I will give the ball to the coach.* p. 57

gloves
Gloves are clothing you wear on your hands to keep them warm. *It was cold outside, so I wore my gloves.* p. 19

glue
a. Glue is a sticky liquid. It is used to stick things like paper together. *We used paper, glue, scissors, and crayons for the art project.* p. 42
b. Glue means to attach one thing to another. *When the frame broke, I needed to glue the pieces together.* p. 57

go
(goes, gone, went)
Go means to move from one place to another. *I want to go with you.* p. 57

goat
A goat is an animal that lives on a farm. A goat is a mammal. Some goats have horns. *He pet the goat at the petting zoo.* p. 8

gobble	A turkey is a large bird. "Gobble-gobble" is the sound a turkey makes. *I heard a turkey say "**gobble-gobble**."* p. 5
goldfish	A goldfish is an animal. A goldfish is a fish. It is small and orange. Some people have a goldfish as a pet. A goldfish lives in a bowl or an aquarium. *Anna feeds her **goldfish** every day.* p. 14
good	Good means nice. Good means safe or correct. *That is a **good** book for kids.* p. 26
goose/ geese	A goose is an animal. A goose is a bird that can fly and swim. Two or more of these birds are called geese. Geese are white or gray and say "honk-honk." *The **goose** waddled across the grass.* p. 6
gorilla	A gorilla is an animal that lives in the jungle. A gorilla is a mammal. A gorilla is the largest monkey. *The **gorilla** ate a banana.* p. 12
grandfather	A grandfather is a person in a family. A grandfather is a mother's father or a father's father. *It is fun to play with my **grandfather**.* p. 28
grandmother	A grandmother is a person in a family. A grandmother is a mother's mother or a father's mother. *My **grandmother** likes to read to me.* p. 28
grapes	Grapes are a fruit. They are small and round. Grapes grow in bunches on vines. Grapes can be green or purple. *Sometimes I eat **grapes** for a snack.* p. 30
grass	Grass is a plant that covers part of the ground. Grass is green and made up of tiny blades. *He mowed the **grass** on Saturday.* p. 40
grasshopper	A grasshopper is an insect. A grasshopper can hop very high. *The **grasshopper** jumped onto the step.* p. 11
grater	A grater is a tool you use in the kitchen. A grater has sharp holes. A grater cuts food into tiny pieces. *The cook used the **grater** to cut up the cheese for the tacos.* p. 22
gray	Gray is a color. Elephants are gray. ***Gray** clouds were in the sky before it rained.* p. 20
green	Green is a color. Grass is green. *I colored the leaves **green**.* p. 20

grocery store	A grocery store is a place where you buy food. *We went to the **grocery store** to buy milk and bread.* p. 38
grow (grew)	When people, plants, and animals grow, they get bigger. *Children **grow** until they are adults.* p. 57
grrr	"Grrr" is a sound that many animals make. "Grrr" is called growling. *The dog said "**Grrr**" when he saw the stranger.* p. 5
guilty	Guilty is a feeling Some people feel guilty when they do something wrong. *I feel **guilty** because I broke your favorite toy.* p. 29
guitar	A guitar is a musical instrument. A person moves the strings on a guitar to play it. *The teacher played the **guitar** while the children sang a song.* p. 35

hail   Hail is balls of ice that sometimes fall from the sky during a storm. *The **hail** that fell last night in the storm broke a window.* p. 65

hair   Hair is part of your body. Hair grows on the top of your head. Hair can be many different colors. *I brush my **hair** every day.* p. 16

ham   Ham is food. Ham is meat. We get ham from pigs. *I ate a **ham** sandwich yesterday.* p. 33

hamburger   A hamburger is food. A hamburger is meat. You usually eat a hamburger on a bun. We get hamburger meat from cows. *We are going to have **hamburgers** for supper tonight.* p. 33

hammer   a. A hammer is a tool. People hit nails with a hammer. *Put the **hammer** in the toolbox.* p. 48
                         b. Hammer means to hit a nail with a tool. *I **hammer** the nail.* p. 57

hamster   A hamster is an animal. A hamster is a mammal. It is small and furry. Some people have a hamster as a pet. *Rosa's class has two **hamsters** in a cage.* p. 14

hand   A hand is part of your body. A person has two hands. Hands are on the ends of your arms. *I clap my **hands**.* p. 16

happy   Happy is a feeling. People smile when they are happy. *When I play with my friend, I am **happy**.* p. 29

hard   a. Hard means not soft. *A pillow is soft. A rock is **hard**.* p. 26
                         b. Hard means not easy. *The math homework is easy. The English homework is **hard**.* p. 26

harmonica   A harmonica is a musical instrument. A harmonica is small and flat. You play a harmonica by blowing into it. *The boy played the **harmonica** as he walked down the street.* p. 35

hat   A hat is a piece of clothing. You wear a hat on your head. *I need to wear a **hat** when it is cold outside.* p. 19

have   Have means to own something. *I **have** a computer at my house.* p. 57
(has, had)

he   He tells about a boy or a man. ***He** walked the dog.* p. 41

head
A head is part of your body. Your head is at the top of your body. Your head has hair, eyes, a nose, a mouth, and ears on it. *The girl nodded her **head**.* p. 17

hear
(heard)
Hear means to listen to a sound with your ears. *I **hear** a radio playing music.* p. 57

hee-haw
A donkey is an animal. "Hee-haw" is the sound a donkey makes. *The donkey brayed "**hee-haw**."* p. 5

heel
A heel is part of your foot. It is the back part of your foot. People have two heels. *I stepped on a rock and hurt my **heel**.* p. 17

helicopter
A helicopter is a way to travel. A person flies in a helicopter. A helicopter has a propeller on the top of it, and it can fly straight up and down. It can also hover, or stay in one place while it is flying. *Sometimes police officers ride in a **helicopter**.* p. 51

help
Help means to do something useful for someone else. *I will **help** my mother wash the dishes.* p. 58

hen
A hen is an animal. A hen is a bird. A hen is a female chicken that lays eggs. *There were many **hens** on the farm.* p. 8

her
a. Her tells about a girl or a woman. *Give the ball to **her**.* p. 70
b. Her means something belongs to a girl or a woman. ***Her** coat is red.* p. 41

hexagon
A hexagon is a shape. A hexagon has six sides. *He drew a **hexagon** on the paper.* p. 45

hide
(hid)
Hide means out of sight. When a person hides, no one can see her. *I will get the tree and **hide** from my friends.* p. 58

high
High means a long way up. *Kites go **high** in the air.* pp. 26, 68

him
Him tells about a boy or a man. *I will sit next to **him**.* p. 70

hippopotamus
A hippopotamus is an animal. A hippopotamus is a mammal. A hippo is very large and lives near water. *Sometimes people say "hippo" instead of **hippopotamus**.* p. 12

his
His means something belongs to a boy or a man. *That is **his** book.* p. 41

hit
Hit means to touch hard with a lot of force. ***Hit** the ball with the bat.* p. 58

hold
(held)
Hold means to take and keep in your hands or arms. *I will **hold** the box for you.* p. 58

home
A home is where someone lives. A house is also a home. *I go **home** after school.* p. 37

honk
a. A goose is an animal. "Honk-honk" is the noise a goose makes. *I heard the geese **honk** as they flew overhead.* p. 5
b. Sometimes people make a noise with car horns. "Honk" is the noise a car horn makes. *I jumped when I heard the car horn "**honk**."* p. 58

hope
Hope means to wish something will happen. *I **hope** I will see my grandmother tomorrow.* p. 29

horse
A horse is an animal. A horse is a mammal. *I can ride a **horse**.* p. 8

hospital
A hospital is a place. A hospital is where sick people go to get better. *Many doctors and nurses work at a **hospital**.* p. 38

hot
Hot means very warm. *Be careful! The stove is very **hot**.* p. 26

hot air balloon
A hot air balloon is a way to travel. A hot air balloon floats up in the sky. People ride in a big basket that hangs from the hot air balloon. *I have never ridden in a **hot air balloon**.* p. 51

hot dog
A hot dog is food. A hot dog is meat. You usually eat a hot dog on a bun. *I ate a **hot dog** at the baseball game.* p. 33

house
A house is a building where someone lives. It has a kitchen, a bathroom, bedrooms, and a living room. A house also has a roof, windows, and doors. *The Perez family lives in the blue **house**.* p. 37

hummingbird
A hummingbird is an animal. A hummingbird is a very small bird. It can stay in one spot, just like a helicopter. A hummingbird drinks nectar from flowers. *The **hummingbird** flew to the flower.* p. 6

hurricane
A hurricane is a very big storm with lots of wind and rain. Hurricanes start in the ocean. *We had to leave the house because a **hurricane** was coming.* p. 65

hurt
Hurt means to feel pain. *I **hurt** my toe when I tripped over the chair.* p. 58

husband
A husband is a person. A husband is a married man. *My aunt's **husband** is my uncle.* p. 28

I   I is a word people use to talk about themselves. *Anna said, "I like to swim."* p. 41

ice   Ice is frozen water. Ice is very hard and very cold. *I make **ice** by putting water into the freezer.* p. 65

ice cream   Ice cream is food. Ice cream is a dessert. Ice cream is sweet and cold. *I like to eat chocolate **ice cream** in the summer.* p. 23

in   a. In means inside. *We went **in** after recess.* p. 68 (See picture for *inside*.)
b. In means to place inside. *Put the ball **in** the box.* p. 68

indoors   Indoors is inside a house or building. *It was raining, so we let the dog come **indoors**.* p. 68

inside   Inside means indoors. *The children played **inside** because it was too cold outside.* p. 68

into   Into is toward the inside of something. *She poured milk **into** my cup.* p. 68

it   It is used when people are talking about something without using the actual name of the item. *The boy said, "Give **it** to me."* p. 41

jacket A jacket is a piece of clothing. You wear a jacket on top of other clothes. A jacket keeps you warm when it is cold outside. *I put on my jacket before I went outside to play.* p. 19

January January is a month. It is the first month of the year. *New Year's Day is on January 1st.* p. 34

jaw The jaw is part of your body. Your jaw is part of your face. Your jaw opens and closes your mouth. *His jaw was tired after he chewed the gum.* p. 17

jealous Jealous is a feeling. Some people might be jealous of what another person has or can do. *I am jealous because you have a new bike and I do not.* p. 29

jellyfish A jellyfish is an animal that lives in the ocean. A jellyfish does not have legs. *We saw a jellyfish at the aquarium.* p. 9

July July is a month. July is the seventh month of the year. *The United States celebrates its birthday on July 4th.* p. 34

jump Jump means to hop into the air with your feet. *I jump over the rock on the playground.* p. 58

jump rope A jump rope is a toy. It is a rope with handles. A child holds one handle in each hand and throws the jump rope over her head. When the rope hits the ground, the child jumps over it. *We need a jump rope for recess.* p. 49

June June is a month. June is the sixth month of the year. Summer begins in June. *We will go to the beach in June.* p. 34

kangaroo
A kangaroo is an animal. A kangaroo is a mammal. A kangaroo has big back feet and can jump high. Kangaroo babies live in the mother kangaroo's pocket. *A baby **kangaroo** is called a joey.* p. 12

keep
(kept)
Keep means to store in a certain place. *I **keep** my books in my backpack.* p. 58

kick
Kick means to hit with the foot. *I can **kick** a ball hard.* p. 58

king
A king is a person. A king is the ruler of a country. Sometimes a king is a character in a story. Some kings are real and some kings are not real. Usually a king wears a crown. *The story was about a **king** and a queen.* p. 46

kite
A kite is a toy. It comes in different shapes. You hold onto a kite with a long string. You throw a kite into the air so it flies. *It's a windy day so let's go fly a **kite**.* p. 49

kitten
A kitten is an animal. A kitten is a mammal. A kitten is a baby cat. *The **kitten** played with the string.* p. 14

knee
A knee is part of your body. It is in the middle of your leg. A person has two knees. *My legs bend at my **knees**.* p. 17

knife
A knife is a tool for eating. A knife cuts food. *The **knife** is very sharp.* p. 22

know
(knew)
Know means to understand clearly. *I **know** the answer.* p. 58

koala
A koala is an animal that lives in Australia. A koala is a mammal. Koala babies live in the mother koala's pouch. *The **koala** ate leaves in the tree.* p. 12

L

label   A label is something to read. A label is on a jar or a box. A label tells what is inside the jar or box. *Read the directions on the **label**.* p. 47

ladybug   A ladybug is an animal. A ladybug is a very small insect. It is usually red. Ladybug wings have black spots on them. *A **ladybug** landed on my arm.* p. 11

lamb   A lamb is an animal. A lamb is a mammal. A lamb is a baby sheep. *The **lamb** ran to its mother.* p. 8

lamp   A lamp is a piece of furniture. A lamp gives light. *It's dark so please turn on the **lamp**.* p. 31

large   Large means big. *A watermelon is a **large** fruit.* p. 26

last   Last means at the end. *I was the **last** person to get a book.* p. 44

late   Late means not on time. *He was **late** for the movie.* p. 66

laugh   A laugh is a sound you make when something is funny. *I **laugh** when my friend tells a joke.* p. 58

leaf   A leaf is part of a plant or tree. Most of the time a leaf is green. Sometimes a leaf will change colors and fall off the tree. *A **leaf** blew off the tree.* p. 40

leave **(left)**   Leave means to go away from a place or to go out. *I **leave** for school at 7:30.* p. 58

left   Left tells which side. It is the opposite of right. *My **left** arm itches.* p. 70

leg   A leg is part of your body. It is attached to your bottom. A person has two legs. We use our legs for standing or walking. *My **leg** hurt after I fell.* p. 17

lemon   A lemon is a yellow fruit that grows on trees. Lemons are sour. *She made lemonade with real **lemons**.* p. 30

leopard   A leopard is an animal. A leopard is a mammal. A leopard is a large cat with spots on its fur. Most leopards live in the jungle. *We saw a **leopard** at the zoo.* p. 12

let   Let means to allow something to happen. *I **let** my sister play with my toys.* p. 58

letter
    a. A letter is something you write or read. You can write a letter and mail it to someone. Then they can read your letter. *I got a **letter** from my friend.* p. 47
    b. A letter is part of the alphabet. There are 26 letters in the alphabet. *Rico's name begins with the **letter** R.* p. 47

lettuce
    Lettuce is food. Lettuce is a vegetable that has green leaves. A salad usually has lettuce in it. *I put **lettuce** on my sandwich.* p. 53

librarian
    A librarian is a person. A librarian's job is to help people find books in a library. *I asked the **librarian** to help me find a book.* p. 21

library
    A library is a place. A library has many books. A person goes to a library to borrow books. *He found his favorite book at the **library**.* p. 39

lick
    Lick means to move your tongue over something. *I **lick** the lollipop with my tongue.* p. 59

lightning
    Lightning is a flash of electricity in the air. Sometimes people see lightning and hear thunder when there is a storm. *I went inside when I saw the **lightning**.* p. 65

like
    Like is a feeling. If a person likes something, he enjoys it very much. *I **like** to eat pancakes for breakfast.* p. 59

lime
    A lime is a green fruit that grows on trees. A lime is sour. *I made limeade with the **limes**.* p. 30

lion
    A lion is an animal. A lion is a mammal. A lion looks like a large cat. A male lion has fur around his head called a mane. Lions live in Africa. *The **lion** roared.* p. 12

lips
    Lips are part of your body. Lips are part of your face. Lips go around your mouth. You use your lips to kiss, smile, and frown. *She licked her **lips**.* p. 17

list
    A list is something to read. A list has words written in order. Sometimes a list has numbers too. *Maria made a **list** of food to get at the grocery store.* p. 47

little
    Little is not big. *An ant is a **little** insect.* p. 26

live
    Live means to call a place your home. *I **live** in a house with my family.* p. 59

lizard
    A lizard is a reptile. A lizard can be green or brown. A lizard is usually small and has a long tail. *The **lizard** climbed on the wall.* p. 15

loaf	Bread is cooked in a loaf before it is cut into slices. All the slices of bread together in the bag are also called a loaf. *We need to buy a **loaf** of bread.* p. 18
long	Long means not short. *Her hair is very **long**.* p. 26
look	Look means to use your eyes to see something. ***Look** at the picture.* p. 59
lose **(lost)**	Lose means that you can't find something. *I will try not to **lose** my new watch.* p. 59
love	Love is a feeling. Love is a strong, warm feeling that you have for another person or a pet. *I **love** my dog very much.* p. 29
low	Low means down. *In the evening, the sun is **low** in the sky.* p. 68

magazine   A magazine is something to look at and read. It has a cover and pages with stories and pictures. *Two **magazines** came in the mail.* p. 47

mail carrier   A mail carrier is a person. A mail carrier's job is to deliver mail to people at work and at home. *The **mail carrier** brought a package and two letters in the mail today.* p. 21

make (made)   Make means create or cause to happen. *My mother will **make** a cake for my birthday.* p. 59

man/men   A man is a male adult. A father is a man. *Two **men** built our new house.* p. 36

mango   A mango is a fruit. The inside is yellow, sweet, and juicy. Mangos grow on trees. *We cut slices of **mango** to eat.* p. 30

many   Many is a lot. *My sister only has one pencil. I have **many** pencils.* p. 32

March   March is a month. It is the third month of the year. *Spring begins in **March**.* p. 34

marker   A marker is used to write or color pictures. Markers come in many colors. *I need a blue **marker** to color the sky in my picture.* p. 42

May   May is a month. It is the fifth month of the year. *It is usually warm in **May**.* p. 34

me   Me is a word people use to talk about themselves. *Please get **me** a glass of water.* p. 70

measuring cup   A measuring cup is a kitchen tool. You use it to measure ingredients for something you cook or bake. *I used a **measuring cup** to measure the flour for the bread I was making.* p. 22

mechanic   A mechanic is a person. A mechanic's job is to use or fix machines or cars. *Our car will not start so a **mechanic** will fix it.* p. 21

meow   Kittens and cats are animals. "Meow" is the sound a kitten or cat makes. *I heard the cat **meow**.* p. 5

microwave   A microwave is a kind of oven. A microwave cooks food quickly. It needs electricity to work. *I popped popcorn in the **microwave**.* p. 31

milk   Milk is a white drink that comes from a cow. *I like to drink **milk** when I eat cookies.* p. 23

mine	Things that belong to me are mine. *Those shoes are **mine**.* p. 70
mirror	A mirror is made of glass. A person looks into a mirror to see himself. *I look in the **mirror** when I brush my hair.* p. 31
mittens	Mittens cover hands to keep them warm. Mittens cover your fingers with a special place for your thumb. *I wear **mittens** when I play in the snow.* p. 19
Monday	Monday is a day of the week. *I have soccer practice on **Monday**.* p. 24
monkey	A monkey is an animal. A monkey is a mammal. Monkeys live in trees and eat bananas. *The **monkey** climbed the tree.* p. 13
moo	A cow is an animal. "Moo" is the sound a cow makes. *I heard the cows **moo** in the barn.* p. 5
mop	a. A mop is used to clean the floor. A mop has a long handle with strings or a sponge at the end. *The floor is dirty so I will use the **mop** to clean it.* p. 31 b. Mop means to clean the floor. *The floor is dirty so I will **mop** it.* p. 59
morning	Morning is a time of day. Morning begins when the sun comes up and ends at noon. *I eat breakfast in the **morning**.* p. 66
mosquito	A mosquito is a flying insect. A mosquito bites animals and people. *There was a **mosquito** buzzing around my ear.* p. 11
mother	A mother is a person in the family. A mother has children. She is a boy's or girl's parent. Another name for Mother is Mom. *I love my **mother**.* p. 28
motorcycle	A motorcycle is a way to travel. A motorcycle has two wheels and a motor. People ride on motorcycles. *The **motorcycle** zoomed down the street.* p. 51
mouse/mice	A mouse is a small animal with a long tail. A mouse is a mammal. Two or more of these animals are called mice. *I saw a **mouse** in the closet.* p. 13
mouth	A mouth is part of your body. A mouth is on your face. Your mouth helps you eat, drink, and talk. *The pizza was hot and burned my **mouth**.* p. 17
move	Move means to change where something is. *We will **move** the table from the living room to the kitchen.* p. 59

muffin   A muffin is food. A muffin is bread. Sometimes people eat muffins for breakfast. *Ling ate a blueberry* **muffin** *for breakfast.* p. 18

mushroom   A mushroom is a small plant. A mushroom is shaped like an umbrella. Some mushrooms are good to eat. *I like* **mushrooms** *on my pizza.* p. 53

my   My means something belongs to me. ***My*** *new shoes are brown.* p. 70

N

nail   A nail is a small, thin piece of metal that is pointed at one end. It is used to hold pieces of wood together. People use a hammer to hit a nail so it goes into wood. *I hung the picture on a **nail**.* p. 48

near   Near means something is close by. *We live **near** the library.* p. 68

neck   A neck is part of your body. A neck connects the head to the body. *I wrapped my scarf around my **neck**.* p. 17

need   Need means you have to have something. *I **need** money to buy things at the store.* p. 59

neigh   A horse is an animal. "Neigh" is the sound a horse makes. *I heard the horse **neigh**.* p. 5

neighborhood   A neighborhood is the area where you live. *There are many houses in my **neighborhood**.* p. 39

never   Never means not ever. *I **never** go to school on Saturday.* p. 66

new   New means not old. *I lost my pencil so I bought a **new** one at school.* p. 26

newspaper   A newspaper is something to read. A newspaper has many pages. *Some people read a **newspaper** every day.* p. 47

next   Next is the one following in order. *It is not my turn yet. There is one person in front of me. I am **next** in line.* p. 44

nickel   A nickel is money. A nickel is a coin. A nickel is worth five cents. *I have a **nickel** in my pocket.* p. 32

night   Night starts when the sun goes down. Night is over when the sun comes up. It is dark at night. *It was ten o'clock at **night**.* p. 66

nine   Nine is a number that comes after eight. *I am **nine** years old.* p. 32

none   None means zero. *I ate all of my cookies. Now I have **none**.* p. 32

nose   A nose is part of your body. It is on your face. You use your nose to smell. You only have one nose. *She needed to blow her **nose**.* p. 17

notebook   A notebook is a book with paper inside. You can write in a notebook. You can put papers in a notebook. *I use a **notebook** at school.* p. 42

November   November is the eleventh month of the year. *My birthday is in **November**.* p. 34

nurse   A nurse is a person. A nurse's job is to take care of sick people. *I saw a **nurse** at the hospital.* p. 21

octagon　　An octagon is a shape. An octagon has eight sides. A stop sign is shaped like an octagon. *I can draw an **octagon**.* p. 45

October　　October is the tenth month of the year. It starts to get cooler in October. *In **October**, we are going to buy pumpkins.* p. 34

octopus　　An octopus is an animal that lives in the ocean. An octopus has eight legs called tentacles. *We saw an **octopus** at the aquarium.* p. 9

off　　a. Off means not on. *The light is not on. I turned it **off**.* p. 26
　　b. Off means not on top of. *The dog jumped **off** the chair.* p. 68

office　　An office is a place. Some people work in an office. People may talk on the telephone or use a computer in an office. *Dan works in an **office**.* p. 39

oink　　A pig is an animal. "Oink" is the sound a pig makes. *Did you hear that pig **oink**?* p. 5

okra　　Okra is a food. Okra is a green vegetable. *I like to eat **okra**.* p. 53

old　　Old means not new. *I have had my shoes for a long time. My shoes are **old**.* p. 26

on　　a. On means not off. *The light is not off. I turned it **on**.* p. 27
　　b. On means on top of. *Put the book **on** the table.* p. 68

one　　One is a number that comes before two. *I lost **one** of my gloves.* p. 32

onion　　An onion is a food. An onion is a vegetable. Onions may be white, yellow, red, or purple. *I like **onion** on my hamburger.* p. 53

open　　Open means not closed. *The door is closed. I will **open** it for you.* p. 59

opossum　　An opossum is an animal. An opossum is a small mammal. It has fur and a long tail. *I saw an **opossum** in the forest.* p. 10

orange　　a. An orange is a fruit. Oranges are round and they grow on trees. You peel an orange before you eat it. *The **orange** tasted good.* p. 30
　　b. Orange is a color. A pumpkin is orange. *I used my **orange** crayon to color the pumpkin.* p. 20

ostrich　　An ostrich is an animal. An ostrich is a big bird. It has a long neck and long legs. An ostrich cannot fly. *An **ostrich** can run fast.* p. 6

our   Our means something belongs to us. *Our school is 25 years old.* p. 41

out   Out means not in. *I took the book out of my backpack.* p. 69

outdoors   Outdoors means under the sky, outside a building. *We did not eat in the house. We ate outdoors.* p. 69

outside   Outside means outdoors. *The dog was in the house, but he wanted to go outside.* p. 69

oval   Oval is a shape like an egg. *My face is an oval shape.* p. 45

over   Over means above something else. *I can jump over the rock.* p. 69

owl   An owl is an animal. An owl is a large bird that flies fast. An owl sleeps during the day and hunts at night. *Sometimes I hear an owl hoot at night.* p. 6

P

paint
    a. Paint is the liquid color used for painting. It comes in a can or a jar. *I dipped my brush in the **paint**.* p. 48
    b. Paint means to use liquid colors and a brush to create a picture. *I like to **paint** pictures.* p. 59

painter
    a. A painter is a person. A painter's job is to paint the outside or the inside of buildings. *The **painter** painted the house green.* p. 21
    b. A painter is another name for an artist. An artist paints pictures that are hung on walls. *The **painter** finished her picture.* p. 59

pajamas
    Pajamas are clothes to sleep in. People wear pajamas when they go to bed. *When I wake up, I take off my **pajamas** and put on clothes for school.* p. 19

pancake
    A pancake is food. It is made of batter and cooked in a frying pan or on a griddle. A pancake is round. *I like to eat **pancakes** for breakfast.* p. 18

panda
    A panda is an animal. A panda is a mammal. A panda is black and white. *The children saw a **panda** at the zoo.* p. 13

pants
    Pants are clothes. They cover your bottom and legs. *She wore **pants** and a sweater.* p. 19

paper
    Paper is made from wood. You can write and draw on paper. You can cut and glue paper. *The teacher gave each student a sheet of **paper**.* p. 42

parakeet
    A parakeet is an animal. A parakeet is a bird. Some people have a parakeet for a pet. *Her **parakeet** lives in a birdcage.* p. 6

park
    A park is a place. A park has trees. A park has a playground. *We will have a picnic at a **park**.* p. 39

parrot
    A parrot is an animal. A parrot is a bird. Some people have a parrot for a pet. *He taught his **parrot** to talk.* p. 7

pastry brush
    A pastry brush is a kitchen tool. You use a pastry brush to spread liquids on foods. *The cook brushed the pie with a **pastry brush**.* p. 22

peach
    A peach is a round fruit. The outside of a peach is fuzzy. Peaches grow on trees. *He ate a **peach** for his snack.* p. 30

peacock
    A peacock is an animal. A peacock is a bird. A peacock has beautiful feathers on its tail. *The **peacock** ate some seeds.* p. 7

pear

A pear is a fruit. Pears are yellow, green, or red. Pears grow on trees. *I chose a **pear** from the fruit bowl.* p. 30

peas

Peas are a food. Peas are small vegetables. Peas are green or black. They grow in a shell called a pod. *We bought **peas** at the grocery store.* p. 53

peeler

A peeler is a kitchen tool. You use a peeler to take the skin off fruits and vegetables. *He scraped the carrots with a **peeler**.* p. 22

pelican

A pelican is an animal. A pelican is a bird with a very large beak. A pelican lives by the ocean and eats fish. *I saw a **pelican** on the beach.* p. 7

pen

A pen is a writing tool. It has ink in it. You use a pen to write on paper. *I got a **pen** and some paper to write a letter.* p. 42

pencil

A pencil is a writing tool. It has lead in it. You use a pencil to write on paper. You can erase pencil marks from paper. *I sharpened my **pencil**.* p. 42

penguin

A penguin is an animal. A penguin is a bird. A penguin is black and white. A penguin cannot fly. *The **penguin** ate some fish.* p. 7

penny

A penny is money. A penny is a coin. A penny is worth one cent. *He has one **penny** and one dime.* p. 32

pentagon

A pentagon is a shape. A pentagon has five sides. *He drew a **pentagon** on the paper.* p. 45

petal

A petal is a part of a flower. Petals can be many colors. *A sunflower has yellow **petals**.* p. 40

piano

A piano is a musical instrument. A piano has 88 black and white keys. You play a piano by pushing down on the keys. *Joe played a song on the **piano**.* p. 35

pig

A pig is an animal. A pig is a mammal. A pig says "oink." *The **pig** rolled in the mud.* p. 8

pigeon

A pigeon is an animal. A pigeon is a bird. *The **pigeon** flew over the building.* p. 7

pineapple

A pineapple is a food. A pineapple is a large fruit. It has rough skin and leaves. You eat the inside of the pineapple. *She put **pineapple** in the fruit salad.* p. 30

pink	Pink is a color. You make pink by mixing red and white paint together. Lips are pink. *I painted the pig **pink**.* p. 20
pirate	A pirate is a character in some stories. A pirate is not real. *In the story, the **pirate** traveled on a ship and stole from people.* p. 46
pita	Pita is a food. Pita is a kind of bread. *You can put meat or vegetables in **pita** bread to make a sandwich.* p. 18
plant	a. A plant needs water, sun, and air to grow. Some plants make flowers. Some plants make fruit or vegetables. *His garden has many **plants** in it.* p. 40
	b. Plant means to put seeds into dirt so they will grow. *She will **plant** corn in the garden.* p. 59
play	a. A play is a story that people act out on a stage. People watch a play. *My class went to see a **play**.* p. 39
	b. Play means to do something for fun. *I like to **play** with my toys.* p. 60
play dough	Play dough is a toy. Children squeeze and roll play dough. Play dough is like clay. *I made a snake out of **play dough**.* p. 49
pliers	Pliers are a tool. Pliers have two handles. Adults use pliers to hold or bend things. *He put the **pliers** in his toolbox.* p. 48
plum	A plum is a round fruit. Plums are purple or red. Plums grow on trees. *A **plum** is a good snack.* p. 30
point	Point means to use your finger to show where something is. ***Point** to the one you want.* p. 60
police officer	A police officer is a person. A police officer's job is to keep people safe. A police officer will help you if you need help. *The **police officer** got out of the car.* p. 21
pony	A pony is an animal. A pony is a mammal. A pony is a little horse. *He can ride his **pony**.* p. 8
porcupine	A porcupine is an animal. A porcupine is a mammal. A porcupine has sharp points called quills on its body. *I will not touch a **porcupine**.* p. 13

pork chop   A pork chop is a food. A pork chop is meat. *He had a **pork chop** and salad for dinner.* p. 33

post office   A post office is a place. People get mail at a post office. You can also buy stamps and mail packages at a post office. *I went to the **post office** to mail a package.* p. 39

potato   A potato is a food. A potato is a vegetable. A potato grows under the ground. Potatoes can be brown or red. *French fries are made from **potatoes**.* p. 53

potato masher   A potato masher is a kitchen tool. You mash potatoes with a potato masher. *Sid used a **potato masher** to make the potatoes smooth.* p. 22

pour   Pour means to make a liquid flow. *I will **pour** milk into my glass.* p. 60

power drill   A power drill is an electric tool. Adults use a power drill to make holes in wood. A power drill makes a loud noise. *He drilled a hole with the **power drill**.* p. 48

present   A present is a gift. A present has wrapping paper and ribbon on it. People give presents to each other. *My friend gave me a **present** for my birthday.* p. 37

pretty   Pretty is good looking or nice to look at. *I like to look at **pretty** flowers.* p. 27

pretzel   A pretzel is a crunchy food. A pretzel is a bread. *I had **pretzels** for my snack.* p. 18

prince   A prince is the son of a king. A prince may be real. A prince may be a character in a story. *The **prince** rode on a white horse.* p. 46

princess   A princess is the daughter of a queen. A princess may be real. A princess may be a character in a story. *The **princess** lived in a castle.* p. 46

print   Print means to write letters. *I can **print** my name on the paper with a pencil.* p. 60

proud   Proud is a feeling. People feel proud when they do something well. *I did a good job. I am **proud** of my work.* p. 29

pull   Pull means to hold something and move it toward yourself. *I **pull** on my shoelaces to tie my shoes.* p. 60

puppet	A puppet is a toy. A puppet can look like a real person or animal but it is made out of cloth, plastic, or wood. *I can make the **puppet** talk.* p. 50
puppy	A puppy is an animal. A puppy is a mammal. A puppy is a baby dog. *The **puppy** likes to chase the cat.* p. 14
purple	Purple is a color. You can make purple by mixing blue and red paint. Some grapes are purple. *I wore a **purple** shirt yesterday.* p. 20
push	Push means to move something away from yourself. *I **push** on the door to close it.* p. 60
put	Put means to move something to a place. *I **put** the fruit in a bowl.* p. 60
puzzle	A puzzle is a toy. A puzzle has many pieces to take apart and put together again. *He chose a **puzzle** from the shelf.* p. 50

quack   A duck is an animal. "Quack" is the sound a duck makes. *I heard the duck* **quack** *when we were throwing bread.* p. 5

quarter   A quarter is money. A quarter is a coin. A quarter is worth 25 cents. *She has a* **quarter** *in her pocket.* p. 32

queen   A queen is a person. A queen is the ruler of a country. Sometimes a queen is a character in a story. Some queens are real and some queens are not real. Usually a queen wears a crown. *The* **queen** *was beautiful and kind.* p. 46

rabbit   A rabbit is an animal. A rabbit is a mammal. A rabbit has long ears and can hop. *Jeff has a pet **rabbit**.* p. 14

raccoon   A raccoon is an animal. A raccoon is a mammal. A raccoon has gray and black fur and it looks like it is wearing a black mask. *We saw a **raccoon** when we went camping.* p. 10

radish   A radish is a food. A radish is a vegetable. A radish is red on the outside and white on the inside. A radish grows under the ground. *I don't like **radishes** in my salad.* p. 53

rain   Rain is water that falls from the clouds to the earth. Rain often falls during a storm. Rain makes plants grow. *The **rain** made our yard muddy.* p. 65

rat   A rat is an animal. A rat is a mammal. A rat has a long tail. A rat likes to chew on things. *The farmer saw a **rat** in the barn.* p. 13

read   Read means to look at words and understand what they mean. *I like to **read** books.* p. 60

recipe   A recipe is something to read. A recipe explains how to make foods. *We followed the **recipe** to make brownies.* p. 47

rectangle   A rectangle is a shape. A rectangle is a box. A rectangle has two long sides and two short sides. A door is shaped like a rectangle. *My teacher asked me to draw a **rectangle**.* p. 45

red   Red is a color. Blood is red. ***Red** is my favorite color.* p. 20

refrigerator A refrigerator is in a kitchen. It keeps food cold. *Milk needs to be kept in a **refrigerator**.* p. 31

reindeer   A reindeer is an animal. A reindeer is a mammal. It has two horns on its head. *Some **reindeer** live at the zoo.* p. 13

rest   Rest means to stop and relax. *When I am tired, I sit down and **rest**.* p. 60

restaurant   A restaurant is a place. You go to a restaurant to eat food. *I looked at the menu when we were at the **restaurant**.* p. 39

rhinoceros   A rhinoceros is a big animal. A rhinoceros is a mammal. It has a horn on its head and lives near water. *"Rhino" is a short name for a **rhinoceros**.* p. 13

ribbit	A frog is an animal. "Ribbit" is the sound a frog makes. *The frog gave a loud "**ribbit**" before he jumped into the water.* p. 5
ride (rode)	Ride means to sit on a vehicle or animal as it moves. *I know how to **ride** a bicycle.* p. 60
right	Right tells which side. It is the opposite of left. *My **right** shoe came off.* p. 70
robin	A robin is an animal. A robin is a bird. A robin has an reddish-orange breast. *You usually see a **robin** in the spring.* p. 7
rocket	A rocket is a way to travel into space. *The **rocket** flew straight up into the sky.* p. 52
roll	a. A roll is food. A roll is bread. *I like butter on my **roll**.* p. 18 b. Roll means to move by turning over and over like a ball. *The ball can **roll** on the floor.* p. 60
rooster	A rooster is an animal. A rooster is a bird. A rooster is a boy chicken. You usually see a rooster on a farm. *The **rooster** crowed loudly.* p. 8
root	A root is the part of a plant that grows under the dirt. Roots help plants get water. Roots keep plants in the ground. *Flowers have **roots**.* p. 40
ruler	A ruler is a tool. You use a ruler to measure things. A ruler is 12 inches long. *I used a **ruler** to measure the paper.* p. 42
run (ran)	Run means to move faster than walking. *I can **run** fast.* p. 60

Ssss   A snake is an animal. "Ssss" is the sound a snake makes. *The snake made a "ssss" sound as it went through the grass.* p. 5

sad   Sad is a feeling. People feel sad when they get hurt or can't have something they want. *My friend moved away so I am sad.* p. 29

sail   a. Some boats have sails. A sail looks like a big triangle. Wind blows on a sail to move the boat. *The man raised the sail on the boat.* p. 52
b. Sail means to move over the water on a boat. *I can sail on the water in a boat.* p. 61

sailboat   A sailboat is a way to travel. A sailboat has a sail. You ride in a sailboat on the water. *We went out on the lake in our new sailboat.* p. 52

sailfish   A sailfish is an animal. A sailfish is a fish. It lives in the ocean. A sailfish has a big fin on its back that looks like a sail. *I saw a sailfish at the aquarium.* p. 9

salamander   A salamander is an animal. A salamander is an amphibian. It looks like a lizard. Salamanders live near water. *Mike caught a salamander by the pond.* p. 15

salmon   a. Salmon is a food. *Some people eat salmon.* p. 33
b. A salmon is an animal. A salmon is a fish. Salmon live in rivers. *My uncle caught a salmon on his fishing trip.* p. 9

Saturday   Saturday is a day of the week. We do not go to school on Saturday. *My piano recital is next Saturday.* p. 24

sausage   Sausage is a food. Sausage is meat. Adults cook sausage in a frying pan. *Some people eat sausage for breakfast.* p. 33

saw   a. A saw is a tool. An adult uses a saw to cut wood. A saw is very sharp. *I watched my dad cut the wood with a saw.* p. 48
b. Saw means to cut with a tool. *I will saw the wood and cut it in two pieces.* p. 61

saxophone   A saxophone is a musical instrument. A saxophone is shaped like the letter "J." You blow into a saxophone to make music. *My brother plays the saxophone.* p. 35

say
(said)   Say means to pronounce words. When you talk, you say words. *When I introduce myself, I say my name.* p. 61

scare   Scare means to frighten. *A loud noise may scare me.* p. 61

school   A school is a place. Children go to school to learn new things. *I can walk to my school.* p. 39

scraper   A scraper is a kitchen tool. People use a scraper to get food out of a bowl. *I like to lick the scraper when my mom bakes a cake.* p. 22

screw   A screw is kind of like a nail. It is used to hold pieces of wood together. You turn a screw with a screwdriver to push it into the wood. *I handed him the screws one at a time.* p. 48

screwdriver   A screwdriver is a tool. People use screwdrivers to make screws go into wood. *The screwdriver is in my toolbox.* p. 48

seagull   A seagull is an animal. A seagull is a bird that lives near the ocean. Seagulls eat fish. *Seagulls flew around the boat.* p. 7

seal   A seal is an animal. A seal is a mammal that lives near the ocean. A seal swims in the ocean to find food to eat. *I watched the seal eat a fish.* p. 13

second   Second comes after first and before third. *I was the second person in line.* p. 44

see   See means to look at something. You see with your eyes. *I see signs when
(saw)   I look out the windows.* p. 61

seed   A seed is part of a plant. Plants make seeds. You can plant seeds in the ground. Seeds grow new plants. *I helped plant the seeds in our garden.* p. 40

September   September is a month. It is the ninth month of the year. Fall begins in September. *I started school in September.* p. 34

seven   Seven is a number. It comes after six. *My brother is seven years old.* p. 32

sew   Sew means to fasten two pieces of cloth together with a needle and thread. *Kate will sew a new dress.* p. 61

shark   A shark is an animal. A shark is a fish that lives in the ocean. A shark has sharp teeth. A shark is very dangerous. *The shark was in a big tank at the aquarium.* p. 9

sharp	Sharp means having an edge or point that can cut easily. *The knife was very **sharp***. p. 27
she	She tells about a girl or a woman. ***She** is a new student in our class.* p. 41
sheep	A sheep is an animal. A sheep is a mammal. Sheep have fur called wool. Sheep say "baa." *I saw many **sheep** at the farm.* p. 8
shine	Shine means to make light. *It will not rain today. The sun will **shine**.* p. 61
ship	A ship is a way to travel. A ship carries many people on the ocean. *The **ship** will take us across the ocean.* p. 52
shirt	A shirt is a type of clothing. It covers your back and your chest. Some shirts have sleeves and some have no sleeves. *My **shirt** has stripes on it.* p. 19
shoes	Shoes are coverings for your feet. Shoes are made out of leather or cloth. You wear shoes to protect your feet. *I keep my **shoes** in the closet.* p. 19
short	Short means not tall or small in height. *I am not tall. I am **short**.* p. 27
shorts	Shorts are a type of clothing. Shorts are like pants but with short legs. You usually wear shorts when it is hot outside. *I wear **shorts** in the summer.* p. 19
shoulder	Your shoulder is the part of your body. It is between your neck and your arms. A person has two shoulders. Your shoulders help your arms move. *The teacher put her hand on the boy's **shoulder** to get his attention.* p. 17
shovel	A shovel is a tool. A shovel has a long handle. You use a shovel to dig a hole in the ground or to move snow. *The **shovel** is in the garage.* p. 61
show	Show means to explain by doing. *Watch me. I will **show** you how to jump rope.* p. 61
shrimp	A shrimp is an animal that lives in the ocean. A shrimp is a crustacean. A shrimp has a shell. ***Shrimp** are good to eat.* p. 9
sign	A sign is something to read. A sign tells people what to do. *The **sign** said "Keep Out."* p. 47
sing **(sang)**	Sing means to make music with your voice. *I like to **sing** songs at school.* p. 61

sink	A sink is a place to wash dishes. A sink is also a place to wash your hands and face. A sink is in a kitchen or a bathroom. *She washed the lettuce in the sink.* p. 31
sister	A sister is a person in a family. A sister is a girl. Sisters and brothers are part of the same family. *My sister is older than my brother.* p. 28
sit **(sat)**	Sit means to rest on your bottom. *I sit in a chair to eat.* p. 61
six	Six is a number. It comes after five. *My brother has six books.* p. 32
skate	a. A skate is a shoe with a blade or wheels on the bottom. Skates help you move on ice or on the sidewalk. *I got new skates for my birthday.* p. 50 b. Skate means to move wearing skates. *I like to skate on the sidewalk.* p. 61
skateboard	A skateboard is a toy. A skateboard has wheels. You stand on a skateboard and make it move. *He rode his skateboard on the sidewalk.* p. 50
skirt	A skirt is a type of clothing. A skirt goes around a girl's waist. Some skirts are long and some are short. *My skirt is in the dryer.* p. 19
skunk	A skunk is an animal. A skunk is a mammal that is black and white. A skunk makes a bad smell. *I don't like the way a skunk smells.* p. 10
sleep **(slept)**	Sleep means to rest with your eyes shut. *I sleep at night.* p. 62
sleet	Sleet is frozen rain. *Sometimes sleet falls from the sky when it is cold.* p. 65
slice	a. A slice is one piece. *I want one slice of bread.* p. 18 b. Slice means to cut with a knife. *Uncle Jim will slice the cheese with a knife.* p. 62
slick	Slick means slippery. *Walk carefully. The wet floor is slick.* p. 27
slide **(slid)**	a. A slide is a playground toy. You climb up a ladder and sit down. Then you go down fast. *I like to play on the slide.* p. 50 b. Slide means to move easily and smoothly. *I like to slide down the hill on my sled.* p. 62
slow	Slow means not fast. *A rabbit is fast. A turtle is slow.* p. 27

small	Small means little. *My brother is not big. He is **small**.* p. 27
smile	A smile is a happy expression. When you smile, the corners of your mouth turn up. *You have a nice **smile**.* p. 62
snake	A snake is an animal. A snake is a long reptile that crawls on the ground. A snake does not have legs. A snake says "ssss." *I saw many **snakes** at the zoo.* p. 15
snow	Snow is ice crystals that fall from the sky. Snow is white. It snows in the winter. *It is fun to play in the **snow**.* p. 65
socks	Socks are a type of clothing. You wear socks on your feet to keep your feet warm. *I couldn't find two **socks** that matched.* p. 19
soft	Soft means easy to shape or smooth to the touch. *Rocks are hard. Pillows are **soft**.* p. 27
son	A son is a person in a family. If a father and mother have a boy child, he is a son. *His **son** is six years old.* p. 28
sorry	Sorry is a bad feeling. People feel sorry if they hurt someone. *I broke your toy. I am **sorry**.* p. 29
sparrow	A sparrow is an animal. A sparrow is a small bird. *The **sparrow** flew to its nest.* p. 7
spatula	A spatula is a kitchen tool. You use a spatula to turn over food like pancakes. *The cook flipped the pancakes with a **spatula**.* p. 22
spoon	A spoon is a kitchen tool. You use a spoon to stir food when it is cooking. You use a spoon to eat soup or cereal. *I eat yogurt with a **spoon**.* p. 22
spring	Spring is a season in the year. In spring, trees get new leaves and flowers bloom. It rains a lot in the spring. ***Spring** begins in March.* p. 43
square	A square is a shape. A square is a box with four equal sides. *This cracker is shaped like a **square**.* p. 45
squash	Squash is a food. Squash is a yellow or green vegetable that grows on a vine. *They grew **squash** in their garden.* p. 53

squirrel	A squirrel is an animal with a bushy tail. A squirrel is a mammal. A squirrel climbs trees and eats nuts. *I saw four **squirrels** at the park.* p. 10
stand **(stood)**	Stand means to be in one place on your feet. *The children have to **stand** in line after recess.* p. 62
starfish	A starfish is an animal. A starfish lives in the ocean. A starfish is shaped like a star. *I found a **starfish** on the beach.* p. 9
start	Start means to begin. *The game will **start** at 7:00.* p. 62
steak	Steak is a food. Steak is meat. *Brian cooked **steak** on the grill.* p. 33
stem	A stem is part of a plant. A stem has leaves on it. Many stems have flowers on them. *Some flowers have long **stems**.* p. 40
stingray	A stingray is an animal. A stingray lives in the ocean. A stingray is shaped like a diamond and has a long tail. *I saw a **stingray** at the aquarium.* p. 9
stir	Stir means to mix up something by moving it around with a stick or utensil. *Dave will **stir** the soup with a big spoon.* p. 62
stomach	The stomach is part of your body. Food and drink go to your stomach when you swallow. *Another name for **stomach** is tummy.* p. 17
stop	Stop means to quit doing something. *When I **stop** talking, I am quiet.* p. 62
storm	A storm is a kind of weather. A storm may bring rain, thunder, and/or lightning. The wind may blow during a storm. *We stayed inside during the **storm**.* p. 65
stove	A stove is used to cook food. A stove is in a kitchen. *The **stove** is hot.* p. 31
strawberry	A strawberry is a fruit. Strawberries are red. Strawberries grow close to the ground. ***Strawberries** are good to eat.* p. 30
stuffed **animal**	A stuffed animal is a toy. A stuffed animal is not a real animal. A stuffed animal can look like a real animal, but it is made of cloth and has stuffing inside it. *I won a **stuffed animal** at the fair.* p. 50
submarine	A submarine is a way to travel. A submarine goes under the water. *I want to ride in a **submarine**.* p. 52

subway   A subway is a way to travel. It is like a train. People in a city ride the subway train underground. *We rode the subway to the museum.* p. 52

summer   Summer is a season in the year. It is usually hot in the summer. *Next summer, I am going to Ohio with my family.* p. 43

sun   The sun is a bright star in the sky. When the sun comes up, it is daytime. When the sun goes down, it is nighttime. *The sun feels warm on my skin.* p. 65

Sunday   Sunday is a day of the week. Sunday is the day before Monday. *On Sunday, we will go on a picnic.* p. 24

surprised   Surprised is a feeling. People feel surprised when something happens that they don't expect. *I was surprised when my friend gave me a present.* p. 29

swan   A swan is an animal. A swan is a bird with white feathers and a long neck. A swan lives near water. *I saw a swan on the pond.* p. 7

sweater   A sweater is a type of clothing. A sweater covers your chest and back and arms. You wear a sweater to keep warm. *Kendra bought a new sweater at the mall.* p. 19

sweep
(swept)   Sweep means to clean with a broom or brush. *You can sweep the floor after dinner.* p. 62

swim
(swam)   Swim means to move through the water. You swim using your arms and legs. Fish swim using their fins and tail. *I like to swim in the pool on a hot day.* p. 62

swing
(swung)   a. A swing is a playground toy. A swing has a seat that hangs by two chains. *I play on the swing at the park.* p. 50
b. Swing means to move back and forth. *I go to the park and swing on the swings.* p. 62

T

T-shirt   A T-shirt is a type of clothing. A T-shirt covers your chest and back. *My T-shirt is orange.* p. 19

table   A table is furniture. A table usually has four legs. You sit at a table to eat. *I put the plates on the table.* p. 31

take   Take means to bring. *I take my backpack to school every day.* p. 62
(took)

talk   Talk means to speak. When you say words to people, you talk. *At school, I raise my hand before I talk.* p. 63

tall   Tall means not short. *That boy is tall.* p. 27

tape   A tape measure is a tool. You use a tape measure to measure things. *Jim*
measure   *used a tape measure to find the length of the table.* p. 48

taxi   A taxi is a way to travel. You pay money to ride in a taxi. Another name for *taxi* is a *cab. We rode in a taxi to the airport.* p. 52

teacher   A teacher is a person. A teacher's job is to help children learn new things. *Mr. Nelson is a teacher.* p. 21

tear   Tear means to rip. *I will help my aunt make a salad. I will tear up the lettuce*
(tore)   *into little pieces for her.* p. 63

telephone   You use a telephone to call someone. You talk on a telephone. *When the telephone rang, I answered it.* p. 31

television   You watch movies and shows on a television. Sometimes it is called a T.V. *She watched the news on television.* p. 31

tell   Tell means to put something into words or to say. *Every day I tell Grandpa*
(told)   *what I did at school.* p. 63

ten   Ten is a number. It comes after nine. *A dime is worth ten cents.* p. 32

thank   Thank means to tell someone you are grateful for something they did or something they gave you. *I thank people when they are nice to me. I say, "Thank you."* p. 63

that   That means the one you are pointing to. *I want that one.* p. 70

their	Their means something belongs to them. *The girls picked up **their** books.* p. 41
them	Them tells about a group of people. *Tell **them** about your school.* p. 70
these	These tells which ones. ***These** books are mine.* p. 70
they	They tells about a group of people. ***They** teach at the same school.* p. 41
think (thought)	Think means to have ideas. People think with their brains. *Do you **think** it will rain today?* p. 63
third	Third comes after second. *This is the **third** book I read today.* p. 44
this	This tells which one. ***This** toy is the one I want.* p. 70
three	Three is a number. It comes after two. *A triangle has **three** sides.* p. 32
throw (threw)	Throw means to send something through the air with your hands. ***Throw** the ball to me.* p. 63
thumb	A thumb is part of your body. You have one thumb on each hand. *The baby sucked her **thumb**.* p. 17
thunder	Thunder is a loud noise. It comes from the sky during a thunderstorm. Sometimes there is lightning when there is thunder. *When I heard **thunder**, I knew it might rain.* p. 65
Thursday	Thursday is a day of the week. *On **Thursday**, I watch my favorite T.V. show.* p. 24
tiger	A tiger is an animal. A tiger is a mammal. A tiger is a large wild cat. A tiger has stripes. *We saw a **tiger** at the zoo.* p. 13
tired	Tired is a feeling. People feel tired after working, exercising, or playing for a long time. *When you feel **tired**, you want to rest.* p. 29
to	To means toward or in a certain direction. *Lisa went **to** the grocery store.* p. 69
toad	A toad is an animal. A toad is an amphibian. Toads live near water. *A **toad** looks like a frog.* p. 15

toast	Toast is a food. Toast is bread that is cooked in a toaster until it is brown. *Aunt Jo put butter on the **toast**.* p. 18
today	Today is this day. *I feel good **today**.* p. 66
toe	A toe is part of your body. A toe is part of your foot. You have five toes on each foot. *It hurt when I hit my **toe** on the chair.* p. 17
toilet	A toilet is in a bathroom. You pee and poop in a toilet. *I always flush the **toilet** when I am done using it.* p. 31
tomorrow	Tomorrow is the day after today. *I cannot go swimming today. I will go swimming **tomorrow**.* p. 66
tongs	Tongs are a kitchen tool. Tongs have handles like scissors. You use tongs to grip and pick up food. *He used **tongs** to turn the meat on the grill.* p. 22
tooth/teeth	A tooth is part of your body. Two or more of these are called *teeth*. You have many teeth in your mouth. Teeth help you chew food. *I go to the dentist twice a year to keep my **teeth** healthy.* p. 17
tornado	A tornado is a big storm. A tornado has high winds that go round and round. *The **tornado** caused lots of damage to the town.* p. 65
tortilla	A tortilla is a Mexican food. A tortilla is a round, flat bread. *I put cheese on my **tortilla**.* p. 18
touch	Touch means to use your hands to feel something. *I use my hands to **touch** things.* p. 63
town	A town is a place where people live and work together. A town is smaller than a city. *Some **towns** have tall buildings.* p. 39
train	A train is a way to travel. A train has an engine and many cars. Many people can ride a train at the same time. *Grandma rode a **train** when she came to visit me.* p. 52
tree	A tree is a plant. A tree has a trunk, branches, and leaves. Trees grow outside. *Some **trees** are very tall.* p. 40
triangle	A triangle is a shape. A triangle has three sides. *A yield sign is shaped like a **triangle**.* p. 45

tricycle   A tricycle is a way to travel. A tricycle has three wheels. The front wheel is big. The two wheels on the back are smaller. You ride a tricycle by pedaling it to make the wheels turn. *Young children ride on **tricycles**.* p. 52

troll   A troll is a character in some stories. A troll is not real. A troll is ugly. A troll is usually the bad guy in a story. *The **troll** hid under the bridge.* p. 46

trombone   A trombone is a musical instrument. You blow into a trombone to make music. *She plays the **trombone** in the school band.* p. 35

truck   A truck is a way to travel. Some trucks are big. Big trucks carry things to stores. *There are many **trucks** on the highway.* p. 52

trumpet   A trumpet is a musical instrument. You blow into a trumpet to make music. *The orchestra had six **trumpet** players.* p. 35

try
(tried)   Try means to attempt or make an effort. *I don't know if I can reach it, but I will **try**.* p. 63

tuba   A tuba is a musical instrument. A tuba is big. You blow into a tuba to make music. *The music teacher brought a **tuba** to class.* p. 35

Tuesday   Tuesday is a day of the week. *On **Tuesday**, I will take my lunch to school.* p. 24

tuna   a. Tuna is a food. *Some people eat **tuna**.* p. 33
         b. A tuna is an animal. A tuna is a fish. ***Tuna** live in the ocean.* p. 9

turkey   a. A turkey is an animal. A turkey is a large bird. Turkeys cannot fly. *I saw **turkeys** on the farm.* p. 8
         b. Turkey is a food. Turkey is meat. *I like to eat **turkey** with potatoes.* p. 33

turn   Turn means to move something in a different direction. *Please **turn** your paper over.* p. 63

turtle   A turtle is an animal. A turtle is a reptile. It has a hard shell. A turtle moves slowly. *I have a pet **turtle**.* p. 15

tweet   A bird is an animal. "Tweet" is the sound a bird makes. *The bird sang "**tweet-tweet**."* p. 5

two   Two is a number. It comes after one. *I have **two** brothers.* p. 32

ugly	Ugly means not pleasant to look at. *I don't like the way the troll looks. He looks **ugly**.* p. 27
uncle	An uncle is a male person in your family. He is your mother's or father's brother. *My **uncle** came for a visit.* p. 28
under	Under means below. *I stand **under** the umbrella to stay dry.* p. 69
underneath	Underneath is below. *Lift up the paper to see what is **underneath** it.* p. 69
unicorn	A unicorn is a character in some stories. A unicorn is not real. A unicorn looks like a horse, but it has one horn on its head. *In the story, the **unicorn** flew away.* p. 46
up	Up means above the ground or a direction. *He is **up** on the ladder. I am down on the ground.* p. 69
upon	Upon means on top of something. *The bird sat **upon** its perch.* p. 69
upstairs	Upstairs is a place. To go upstairs, you must climb up the stairs. *I go up the stairs to get **upstairs**. I go down the stairs to get downstairs.* p. 69
us	Us tells about a group of people. *They invited all of **us** to the party.* p. 70
use	Use means to make something work. *I **use** the telephone to call someone.* p. 63

vest	A vest is a type of clothing. A vest looks like a shirt without sleeves. *I buttoned my **vest**.* p. 19
vine	A vine is a plant with leaves and stems. Some vines are very long. Sometimes vines grow on fences or buildings. *I helped Dad trim the **vine** on the fence.* p. 40
violin	A violin is a musical instrument. A violin has strings. You use a bow to make music on a violin. *The **violin** is my favorite musical instrument.* p. 35

waffle	A waffle is a breakfast food. A waffle is bread. Some people put syrup on waffles. *On Saturday, I had **waffles** for breakfast.* p. 18
wagon	A wagon is a toy. It has a handle and four wheels. You can ride in a wagon or pull a wagon. *I like to pull my sister in the **wagon**.* p. 50
waist	A waist is part of your body. Your waist is between your chest and your hips. *My belt goes around my **waist**.* p. 17
waitress/ waiter	A waitress is a female person who works in a restaurant. A waitress's job is to bring food and drinks to people in the restaurant. *The **waitress** gave me a menu.* p. 21
walk	Walk means to go somewhere using your feet. *I will **walk** to my friend's house.* p. 63
want	Want means to wish for something. *I **want** a new bike.* p. 63
warm	Warm is a temperature between hot and cold. *I kept the food **warm** for you.* p. 27
wash	Wash means to clean with soap and water. *After dinner, I help **wash** the dishes.* p. 64
watch	a. A watch is a small clock. *You wear a **watch** on your arm.* p. 37 b. Watch means to look at. ***Watch** me. I will show you how to do it.* p. 64
water	a. Water is a clear liquid. You drink water. Water is found in oceans, lakes, and ponds. *She wanted a glass of **water**.* p. 37 b. Water means to put water into or on. *I will **water** the plants.* p. 64
watermelon	A watermelon is a large fruit. A watermelon is green on the outside and red on the inside. A watermelon grows on a vine on the ground. ***Watermelon** is my favorite snack in the summer.* p. 30
we	We tells about a group of people. ***We** had hamburgers for dinner.* p. 41
wear (wore)	Wear means you have clothes or jewelry on your body. *In the winter, I must **wear** a coat.* p. 64
Wednesday	Wednesday is a day in the middle of the week. *Evan has soccer practice on **Wednesday**.* p. 24

whale	A whale is a big animal that lives in the ocean. A whale is a mammal. *We studied whales at school.* p. 9
whisk	A whisk is a kitchen tool. You use a whisk to mix things in a bowl. *The chef used a whisk to beat the eggs.* p. 22
whistle	a. A whistle is a small device made of metal or plastic. *You blow on a whistle to make a loud noise.* p. 50 b. Whistle means to make a sound by blowing air through your rounded lips. *When I'm happy, I whistle.* p. 64
white	White is a color. Snow is white. *Some paper is white.* p. 20
whoo	An owl is an animal. "Whoo" is the sound an owl makes. *We heard the owl say "whoo-whoo."* p. 5
wife	A wife is a person. A wife is a woman who is married. *A man is married to his wife.* p. 28
wind	Wind is air that is moving. *I can feel the wind blowing on my face.* p. 65
wink	Wink means to open and close one eye quickly. *I like to wink at my mom.* p. 64
winter	Winter is a season in the year. It is usually cold in the winter. *I like to drink hot chocolate in the winter.* p. 43
wish	Wish means to hope. *I wish I could use the computer.* p. 64
witch	A witch is a character in some stories. A witch is not real. A witch is usually ugly. *In the story, the witch rode on a broom.* p. 46
wizard	A wizard is a character in some stories. A wizard is not real. A wizard can make magic. *The wizard changed the dog into a rock.* p. 46
wolf	A wolf is a wild animal. A wolf is a mammal that looks like a dog. *My teacher read a book about a wolf to my class.* p. 10
woman/ women	A woman is a female adult. A mother is a woman. *Two women came to our door.* p. 36

woodpecker A woodpecker is an animal. A woodpecker is a bird. A woodpecker taps on trees with its beak. *Sometimes I hear a **woodpecker** tapping on the tree outside my window.* p. 7

woof A dog is an animal. "Woof" is the sound a dog makes. *I heard the dog say "**woof**" when we walked by.* p. 5

work
   a. Work is where a person goes to earn money. It is also called a job. *He goes to **work** in his car.* p. 64
   b. Work means to make something or get something done. *I **work** on my papers at school. At recess I can play.* p. 64

wrap Wrap means to cover a gift with paper so you can't tell what the gift is. *I will **wrap** the box with pretty paper.* p. 64

wrench A wrench is a tool. An adult uses a wrench to hold a bolt so he can turn the bolt. *I saw a **wrench** in the garage.* p. 48

wrist A wrist is part of your body. Your wrist is between your hand and your arm. A person has two wrists. *The teacher had a watch on her **wrist**.* p. 17

write
(wrote) Write means to form letters and words on paper using a pen or pencil. *I **write** on paper with a pencil.* p. 64

xylophone   A xylophone is a musical instrument. A xylophone has several metal bars on it. You hit the bars with sticks to make music. *Mike played a **xylophone** at school.* p. 35

yawn   Yawn means to stretch your mouth wide open and breathe in and out when you are tired. *When I am sleepy, I open my mouth and **yawn**.* p. 64

year   A year is 12 months. A year starts on January 1st and ends on December 31st. *I grew three inches last **year**.* p. 66

yell   Yell means to shout loudly. *People like to scream and **yell** at football games.* p. 64

yellow   Yellow is a color. *A banana is **yellow**.* p. 20

yesterday   Yesterday is the day before today. ***Yesterday** I was sick. Today I feel better.* p. 66

yogurt   Yogurt is a food. Yogurt is made from milk. Sometimes yogurt has fruit in it. *You can eat **yogurt** for breakfast or for a snack.* p. 23

you   You is a word for another person. ***You** are a nice person.* p. 41

your   Your means it belongs to the person you are talking to. *This is not my book. This is **your** book.* p. 41

yo-yo   A yo-yo is a toy. A yo-yo is round and has a long string. You hold the string and make the yo-yo go up and down. *Ryan bought a **yo-yo** at the store.* p. 50

Z

zebra   A zebra is an animal. A zebra is a mammal that looks like a horse. A zebra has black and white stripes. *I always see **zebras** at the zoo.* p. 13

zero   Zero is a number. Zero means nothing. *One plus **zero** equals one.* p. 32

19-03-987654321